ARTIFICIAL INTELLIGENCE WILL MAKE US DUMB

COPYRIGHT © CALEBMAINAIDI

2023

ALL RIGHTS RESERVED

TABLE OF CONTENTS

Introduction
1.1 Overview of Artificial Intelligence
1.2 The Role of AI in Modern Society
1.3 Thesis Statement: The Potential Negative Impact of AI on Human Intelligence

Understanding Human Intelligence
2.1 Definition of Human Intelligence
2.2 Cognitive Abilities and Skills
2.3 Importance of Human Intelligence in Problem Solving and Decision Making

The Rise of Artificial Intelligence
3.1 Definition and Types of Artificial Intelligence
3.2 Advancements in AI Technologies
3.3 AI Applications in Various Fields

Potential Negative Effects of AI on Human Intelligence

4.1 Overreliance on AI Systems

4.2 Reduced Cognitive Abilities and Skills

4.3 Loss of Critical Thinking and Problem-Solving Skills

4.4 Implications for Education and Learning

Bias and Limitations in AI Systems

5.1 Bias in AI Algorithms

5.2 Limitations in AI Decision-Making

5.3 Impact on Human Creativity and Innovation

Dependency on AI Technology

6.1 Automation and Job Displacement

6.2 Reduced Need for Memory and Recall

6.3 Effects on Social Interaction and Communication

Ethical Considerations and Challenges

7.1 Privacy and Data Security Concerns

7.2 Ethical Implications of AI Decision-Making

7.3 Human Responsibility in AI Development and Use

8.2 Human-AI Collaboration and Augmentation

8.3 Ethical Frameworks and Regulations

Conclusion

9.1 Recap of the Argument

9.2 Balancing the Benefits and Risks of AI

9.3 Future Perspectives

Recommendations

Introduction

In the modern era, artificial intelligence (AI) has emerged as a powerful tool that has the potential to transform various aspects of our lives. From virtual assistants and self-driving cars to personalized recommendations and predictive analytics, AI has undoubtedly made remarkable strides in enhancing convenience and efficiency. However, as this technology becomes increasingly integrated into our daily routines, concerns have arisen regarding its impact on human intelligence. There is a growing belief among some critics that, rather than augmenting our intellectual abilities, AI has the potential to make us dumb. This provocative viewpoint raises important questions about the effects of AI on human cognition, the nature of intelligence, and our role in a world increasingly driven by intelligent machines. In this essay, we will delve into the arguments surrounding this topic and critically examine the potential ways in which AI might influence human intelligence, for better or worse. By exploring both the potential drawbacks and benefits of AI, we can gain a deeper understanding of its impact on our cognitive abilities and navigate the path forward with greater clarity and caution.

The idea that artificial intelligence will make us dumb stems from a range of concerns and observations. One of the primary arguments put forth is the increasing reliance on AI-powered devices and algorithms to perform tasks that were traditionally handled by human intelligence. As AI systems become more advanced and capable, there is a fear that we may become overly dependent on them, leading to a decline in our own cognitive skills.

Take, for example, the proliferation of virtual assistants like Siri, Alexa, and Google Assistant. These voice-activated AI systems have made it incredibly convenient to access information, perform tasks, and control our devices. However, their omnipresence has raised concerns about the erosion of our critical thinking and problem-solving abilities. Instead of actively engaging our brains to recall information or solve complex problems, we may simply rely on AI assistants to provide us with quick answers and solutions. Over time, this lack of mental exercise could potentially lead to a decline in our cognitive abilities.

Another aspect that contributes to the notion of AI making us dumb is the phenomenon known as the "filter bubble" or "echo chamber." AI algorithms have the capability to personalize content and recommendations based on our preferences and browsing history. While this can enhance user experience and save time, it also creates a bubble around us, reinforcing our existing beliefs and limiting exposure to diverse perspectives. As a result, we may become less open-minded, less informed about alternative viewpoints, and less capable of critically evaluating information.

Furthermore, there is concern about the potential job displacement caused by AI. As AI technology continues to advance, it has the capacity to automate various tasks, leading to the elimination of certain jobs. While this automation can improve efficiency and productivity, it also raises questions about the skills and capabilities humans will need in the future workforce. If individuals are not adequately prepared to adapt to the changing landscape and acquire new skills, there is a risk of a widening knowledge gap and a decline in overall intellectual capacity.

However, it is important to acknowledge that the impact of AI on human intelligence is a complex and nuanced issue. While there are valid concerns, there are also potential benefits that should not be overlooked. AI has the capacity to augment our cognitive abilities, providing tools and insights that can enhance our decision-making processes, improve efficiency, and enable us to tackle more complex problems. Additionally, AI systems can act as valuable educational tools, personalizing learning experiences and providing access to information and resources that were previously inaccessible.

In conclusion, the assertion that artificial intelligence will make us dumb is a contentious and multifaceted topic. While there are concerns about the potential negative impacts of AI on human cognition, it is crucial to consider both the drawbacks and benefits of this technology. By actively engaging in discussions, research, and ethical considerations surrounding AI, we can strive for a balanced approach that maximizes the advantages while mitigating the potential risks. Ultimately, the future relationship between AI and human intelligence will depend on how we navigate and shape this rapidly evolving field.

Overview of Artificial Intelligence

Artificial Intelligence (AI) is a rapidly evolving field that aims to develop intelligent machines capable of performing tasks that typically require human intelligence. Over the years, AI has made significant advancements, with the development of sophisticated algorithms, powerful computing resources, and vast amounts of data. This overview provides a comprehensive understanding of AI, its various subfields, applications, challenges, and ethical considerations.

History of Artificial Intelligence:
The roots of AI can be traced back to ancient civilizations, where myths and folklore depicted artificial beings with human-like intelligence. However, modern AI began to take shape in the 1950s, with the development of early computational models and the establishment of AI as a distinct field of study. Key milestones include the

Dartmouth Conference, the development of expert systems, and the rise of machine learning algorithms.

Types of Artificial Intelligence:
AI can be broadly categorized into two types: Narrow AI and General AI. Narrow AI, also known as weak AI, refers to AI systems designed to perform specific tasks or solve specific problems, such as voice recognition, image classification, or playing chess. General AI, on the other hand, refers to AI systems that possess human-level intelligence and can perform any intellectual task that a human being can do.

Machine Learning:
Machine learning is a subset of AI that focuses on developing algorithms capable of learning from data and improving performance over time. It can be further classified into three types: supervised learning, unsupervised learning, and reinforcement learning. Supervised learning involves training

algorithms using labeled data, while unsupervised learning involves finding patterns in unlabeled data. Reinforcement learning involves training agents to interact with an environment and learn from feedback.

Deep Learning:
Deep learning is a subfield of machine learning that utilizes artificial neural networks with multiple layers to process complex patterns and extract meaningful insights from vast amounts of data. Deep learning has revolutionized several AI applications, including computer vision, natural language processing, and speech recognition. Convolutional Neural Networks (CNNs) and Recurrent Neural Networks (RNNs) are popular architectures in deep learning.

Natural Language Processing (NLP):
NLP focuses on enabling computers to understand, interpret, and generate human language. It involves tasks such as speech recognition, language

translation, sentiment analysis, and chatbots. NLP techniques often leverage machine learning and deep learning algorithms to process and analyze text or speech data.

Computer Vision:
Computer vision aims to enable machines to understand and interpret visual information from images or videos. It involves tasks such as object recognition, image classification, facial recognition, and image segmentation. Deep learning approaches, particularly CNNs, have significantly improved the performance of computer vision systems.

Robotics and Autonomous Systems:
AI plays a crucial role in robotics and autonomous systems, enabling machines to perceive the environment, make decisions, and interact with the physical world. Applications range from industrial robots used in manufacturing to self-driving cars, drones, and humanoid robots. AI techniques,

including computer vision and reinforcement learning, contribute to the development of intelligent robotic systems.

AI in Healthcare:

AI has immense potential in the healthcare industry, with applications in medical imaging analysis, disease diagnosis, drug discovery, personalized medicine, and virtual healthcare assistants. Machine learning algorithms can analyze medical data to detect patterns and make predictions, aiding in early detection and treatment of diseases.

AI in Finance:

AI is transforming the finance industry by automating processes, improving fraud detection, and enhancing investment strategies. Machine learning models can analyze vast amounts of financial data to identify patterns, predict market trends, and optimize trading decisions. AI-powered chatbots and virtual assistants also provide personalized financial advice and customer support.

Ethical Considerations:
The rapid advancement of AI raises various ethical concerns. Issues such as bias in AI systems, privacy and data security, job displacement, and the potential misuse of AI technology need to be addressed. Ethical frameworks and guidelines are being developed to ensure responsible AI development and deployment. It is crucial to prioritize transparency, accountability, fairness, and human-centric values in AI systems.

AI and Society:
The widespread adoption of AI technologies is reshaping various aspects of society. It has the potential to improve productivity, enhance decision-making, and transform industries. However, it also raises concerns about job automation and inequality. It is essential to ensure that AI benefits all members of society, bridging the

digital divide and promoting inclusive development.

AI Governance and Regulation:
Given the potential risks associated with AI, governments and organizations are working on establishing regulatory frameworks to govern AI development and deployment. These frameworks aim to address ethical concerns, protect individuals' rights, and ensure responsible use of AI technologies. International collaborations and partnerships are being formed to foster global AI governance standards.

Future Trends and Challenges:
The field of AI is continuously evolving, and several future trends and challenges are emerging. Some of these include the development of explainable AI, AI for social good, quantum computing's impact on AI, and the integration of AI with other emerging technologies like the Internet of Things (IoT) and blockchain. Ensuring the security and robustness of

AI systems and addressing biases and fairness in AI algorithms will also be critical moving forward.

Artificial Intelligence has transformed from a theoretical concept to a practical reality, revolutionizing various industries and shaping the way we live and work. With advancements in machine learning, deep learning, natural language processing, and computer vision, AI continues to push boundaries and unlock new possibilities. However, it is essential to approach AI development and deployment with ethical considerations and responsible practices to ensure that AI benefits society as a whole. As AI continues to evolve, collaboration, governance, and ongoing research will play crucial roles in shaping its future impact.

The Role of Artificial Intelligence in Modern Society

Artificial Intelligence (AI) has emerged as a transformative force in various aspects of modern society. From revolutionizing industries to enhancing daily life experiences, AI technologies are reshaping the way we live, work, and interact with the world around us. In this comprehensive essay, we will delve into the multifaceted role of AI in modern society, exploring its applications, benefits, challenges, and potential future implications.

AI in Industry and Economy:

1.1 Automation and Robotics: AI is driving automation and robotics to new heights, transforming industries such as manufacturing, logistics, and agriculture. Intelligent machines are replacing manual labor in repetitive tasks, leading to increased efficiency, productivity, and cost-effectiveness.

1.2 Data Analysis and Decision Making: AI-powered analytics and machine learning algorithms are helping businesses make informed decisions by processing vast amounts of data, identifying patterns, and generating valuable insights. This enhances strategic planning, resource allocation, and risk management.

1.3 Customer Experience and Personalization: AI enables personalized recommendations, chatbots, and virtual assistants, enhancing customer experiences in sectors like e-commerce, banking, and healthcare. These technologies improve responsiveness, convenience, and satisfaction levels.

AI in Healthcare:

2.1 Diagnostics and Medical Imaging: AI algorithms excel at analyzing medical images, aiding in the early detection of diseases like cancer and providing accurate diagnoses. This improves patient outcomes, reduces human error, and enhances the efficiency of healthcare professionals.

2.2 Drug Discovery and Development: AI algorithms can sift through vast amounts of scientific data, accelerating the drug discovery process and identifying potential treatment options. This has the potential to revolutionize pharmaceutical research and improve patient care.

2.3 Telemedicine and Remote Patient Monitoring: AI-powered telehealth solutions enable remote consultations, real-time monitoring of vital signs, and predictive analytics for early intervention. This expands access to healthcare, especially in underserved areas, and improves patient convenience and engagement.

AI in Transportation and Mobility:

3.1 Autonomous Vehicles: AI is a driving force behind the development of autonomous vehicles, making significant advancements in self-driving technology. This has the potential to reduce accidents, increase transportation efficiency, and revolutionize the way we commute.

3.2 Traffic Management and Optimization: AI algorithms optimize traffic flow, reduce congestion, and improve transportation infrastructure planning. This results in reduced travel times, fuel consumption, and environmental impact.

3.3 Intelligent Transportation Systems: AI enables smart transportation systems, including real-time route planning, predictive maintenance, and demand-responsive services. These systems enhance the overall efficiency and reliability of transportation networks.

AI in Education:

4.1 Personalized Learning: AI-powered educational platforms offer personalized learning experiences, adapting to individual student needs, strengths, and weaknesses. This fosters better engagement, knowledge retention, and academic performance.

4.2 Intelligent Tutoring Systems: AI algorithms can act as virtual tutors, providing immediate feedback, adaptive instruction, and personalized support to learners. This improves learning outcomes and bridges educational gaps.

4.3 Administrative Efficiency: AI streamlines administrative tasks, automating processes such as grading, scheduling, and data analysis. This allows educators to focus more on teaching and student interactions.

AI in Social Media and Communication:

5.1 Natural Language Processing: AI enables natural language processing, facilitating sentiment analysis, language translation, and chatbot interactions. This enhances communication and connectivity across different languages and cultures.

5.2 Social Media Analysis: AI algorithms analyze social media data, identifying trends, sentiment patterns, and user behavior. This helps businesses understand their customers, target their marketing strategies, and manage online reputation.

5.3 Content Moderation and Fake News Detection: AI algorithms play a crucial role in identifying and moderating inappropriate or harmful content on social media platforms.

5.3 Content Moderation and Fake News Detection (continued):

also aid in the detection of fake news and disinformation, helping to maintain the integrity of online information and promoting a safer digital environment.

AI in Entertainment and Media:

6.1 Content Recommendation Systems: AI-powered recommendation systems analyze user preferences and behavior to provide personalized content suggestions across various entertainment platforms, including streaming services, music platforms, and online news outlets. This enhances user experience and engagement.

6.2 Content Creation and Augmentation: AI technologies, such as natural language processing and computer vision, are being used to generate and enhance creative content in areas like music, art, and video production. This pushes the boundaries of human creativity and offers new avenues for artistic expression.

6.3 Virtual Reality and Gaming: AI plays a crucial role in creating realistic virtual environments and intelligent virtual characters in virtual reality (VR) and gaming applications. This enhances immersion, interactivity, and the overall gaming experience.

Ethical Considerations and Challenges:

7.1 Privacy and Data Security: The increasing use of AI raises concerns about the privacy and security of personal data. Striking a balance between data collection for AI applications and protecting individual privacy is a critical challenge for society.

7.2 Bias and Fairness: AI systems are only as good as the data they are trained on. Biases in training data can lead to biased decision-making, perpetuating discrimination and inequality. Ensuring fairness and accountability in AI algorithms is essential.

7.3 Job Displacement and Workforce Transition: The automation capabilities of AI raise concerns about job displacement and the need for upskilling and reskilling the workforce to adapt to new roles and industries. Ensuring a smooth transition and equitable opportunities for workers is crucial.

7.4 Algorithmic Transparency and Explainability: The black-box nature of some AI algorithms makes it difficult to understand their decision-making processes. Ensuring transparency and explainability is important to build trust and prevent algorithmic biases.

7.5 Ethical AI Development and Deployment: Society must address ethical considerations surrounding AI, such as ensuring AI technologies are used for the benefit of humanity, adhering to ethical guidelines, and avoiding malicious uses or unintended consequences.

Future Implications and Possibilities:

8.1 Advancements in AI Research: Continued research and development in AI will lead to breakthroughs in areas like natural language understanding, reasoning, and general intelligence, paving the way for more sophisticated AI systems.

8.2 Human-Machine Collaboration: The future of AI lies in collaboration between humans and machines, leveraging the strengths of both to solve complex problems and create innovative solutions across various domains.

8.3 Ethical AI Governance: Establishing robust governance frameworks, regulations, and standards for the development, deployment, and use of AI will be crucial to ensure responsible and ethical AI adoption.

8.4 Socioeconomic Impact: AI has the potential to reshape economies, industries, and the job market. Society must prepare for these transformations, embracing the opportunities while mitigating the potential negative socioeconomic consequences.

The role of AI in modern society is extensive and diverse. From transforming industries and revolutionizing healthcare to enhancing education and entertainment, AI is a powerful tool that has the potential to drive significant advancements and improvements in various aspects of our lives. However, addressing ethical considerations, ensuring transparency, and managing the societal impact of AI will be essential to harness its full potential while safeguarding the well-being of individuals and society as a whole. With responsible development and deployment, AI can be a force for positive change, enhancing efficiency, productivity, and quality of life in the modern world.

1.3 The Potential Negative Impact of AI on Human Intelligence

Artificial Intelligence (AI) has emerged as a groundbreaking technology with tremendous potential to transform various industries and aspects of human life. While AI offers numerous benefits, such as increased efficiency, improved decision-making, and enhanced problem-solving capabilities, there is a growing concern about its potential negative impact on human intelligence. This article explores the potential risks and adverse effects that AI may pose to human intelligence. It examines areas such as cognitive abilities, emotional intelligence, creativity, social interaction, and ethical considerations. By delving into these topics, we aim to foster a comprehensive understanding of the potential negative implications of AI on human intelligence and initiate a broader discussion on responsible AI development.

Artificial Intelligence and its Significance:

Artificial Intelligence (AI) refers to the development of computer systems capable of performing tasks that typically require human intelligence, such as understanding natural language, recognizing patterns, and making decisions. AI has gained significant traction in recent years, revolutionizing industries like healthcare, finance, transportation, and entertainment.

Defining Human Intelligence:

Human intelligence encompasses a broad range of cognitive abilities, including reasoning, problem-solving, memory, learning, emotional intelligence, and creativity. These abilities are central to human adaptation, innovation, and social interaction.

The Promise of AI:

AI holds immense promise to augment human capabilities, enhance productivity, and address complex challenges. It has the potential to improve decision-making processes, optimize resource allocation, and enable the development of innovative solutions.

Objective of the Article:
While AI offers numerous benefits, there is a growing concern regarding its potential negative impact on human intelligence. This article aims to explore and shed light on the potential risks and adverse effects that AI may pose to human intelligence. By examining various aspects of human intelligence, such as cognitive abilities, emotional intelligence, creativity, and social interaction, we seek to provide a comprehensive understanding of the potential negative implications of AI. Furthermore, we will discuss the ethical considerations associated with AI development and propose strategies to mitigate the negative impact and ensure responsible AI deployment.

The Cognitive Impact of AI on Human Intelligence

2.1. Dependency on AI:

One potential negative impact of AI on human intelligence is the increasing dependency on AI systems for tasks that were traditionally performed by humans. As individuals rely more on AI for decision-making and problem-solving, there is a risk of diminishing cognitive skills and critical thinking abilities. If humans become overly dependent on AI algorithms, their own cognitive capabilities may deteriorate over time, leading to a decline in intellectual capacity.

2.2. Degradation of Critical Thinking:

AI systems are designed to optimize efficiency and accuracy, often relying on vast amounts of data and algorithms to make decisions. While this can lead to more accurate outcomes, it may also result in a reduced emphasis on critical thinking. If individuals rely solely on AI-generated results without questioning or critically analyzing them, their ability to think independently and critically may diminish, affecting their problem-solving skills and intellectual growth.

2.3. Reduced Problem-Solving Skills:
AI's ability to rapidly process information and provide solutions can potentially hinder the development of human problem-solving skills. When individuals rely on AI to provide answers, they may miss out on the opportunity to engage in analytical thinking, creativity, and innovative problem-solving approaches. Over time, this reliance on AI for solutions could lead to a decline in human problem-solving abilities.

2.4. Erosion of Memory:
With the convenience of AI-powered tools and search engines, individuals may rely less on their own memory. Rather than retaining information, individuals may rely on AI systems to retrieve information on-demand. This reliance on external sources for memory retrieval may lead to a decline

in memory capacity and the ability to recall information independently.

2.5. Stagnation of Intellectual Growth:
Human intelligence thrives on continuous learning, exploration, and intellectual growth. However, the ease of accessing information through AI systems may lead to a complacency that inhibits intellectual curiosity and the pursuit of knowledge. If individuals become satisfied with the readily available information provided by AI, there is a risk of stagnation in intellectual growth and a lack of motivation to seek deeper understanding or engage in independent research.

2.6. Superficial Learning:
AI-powered educational tools and platforms have the potential to revolutionize learning by personalizing content and adapting to individual needs. However, there is a concern that AI-driven education may focus on optimizing exam scores and performance metrics rather than fostering deep

understanding and critical thinking. This emphasis on surface-level learning may hinder the development of complex problem-solving skills and comprehensive knowledge acquisition.

The Emotional Impact of AI on Human Intelligence
3.1. Empathy and Emotional Connection:
Emotional intelligence, including empathy and the ability to form meaningful connections with others, is a fundamental aspect of human intelligence. While AI systems can simulate emotions and responses, they lack genuine emotional experiences. Excessive reliance on AI for emotional interactions may lead to a reduced ability to empathize and connect with others on a deeper emotional level.

3.2. Psychological Well-being:
The increasing integration of AI systems in various aspects of life, such as virtual assistants, social media algorithms, and personalized advertisements, raises concerns about the potential

negative impact on psychological well-being. AI algorithms can manipulate user experiences, influence emotions, and create addictive feedback loops that may lead to mental health issues, such as anxiety, depression, and social isolation.

3.3. Emotional Intelligence: AI systems are designed

to analyze and interpret human emotions, but they do not possess emotional intelligence in the same way humans do. Emotional intelligence involves understanding and managing emotions, as well as perceiving and responding to the emotions of others. Excessive reliance on AI for emotional support or decision-making may hinder the development and refinement of emotional intelligence in individuals, leading to a potential decline in their ability to navigate complex social interactions and relationships.

3.4. Loss of Human Touch and Intuition:

Human intuition and instinct play a crucial role in decision-making, particularly in situations where logical reasoning may be insufficient. The reliance on AI systems that rely solely on data-driven algorithms may diminish the importance of human intuition. Over time, individuals may become less attuned to their own instincts and rely solely on AI-generated recommendations, potentially leading to a loss of the human touch in decision-making processes.

3.5. Alienation and Isolation:
The integration of AI systems in social interactions, such as chatbots and virtual companions, may provide a sense of companionship and support. However, excessive reliance on AI for social interactions can lead to a sense of alienation and isolation. Human connections and relationships are essential for personal growth, emotional well-being, and social cohesion. If individuals increasingly substitute human interactions with AI-driven

interactions, there is a risk of social isolation and the deterioration of social intelligence.

The Creativity Impact of AI on Human Intelligence
4.1. Creativity as a Uniquely Human Trait:
Creativity is often considered a hallmark of human intelligence, involving the generation of novel ideas, artistic expression, and problem-solving approaches. While AI systems can generate outputs that mimic creativity, they lack the depth of human creativity, which stems from emotions, experiences, and unique perspectives. Overreliance on AI-generated content and solutions may limit the development and expression of human creativity.

4.2. AI-Generated Content and Originality:
AI technologies, such as generative models and algorithms, have the capability to produce content, including music, art, and literature. While AI-generated content can be impressive, there are concerns about originality and authenticity. If AI-generated content becomes dominant, there is a

risk of diminishing the value placed on human-created works, stifling innovation, and reducing the diversity of artistic expression.

4.3. Diminished Creativity in Problem-Solving:

AI systems excel in analyzing vast amounts of data and providing optimized solutions to well-defined problems. However, they may struggle with creative problem-solving, which often requires thinking outside the box, exploring unconventional approaches, and embracing ambiguity. If individuals rely solely on AI for problem-solving, there is a risk of diminishing their own creative problem-solving abilities.

4.4. Stifling Innovation and Risk-Taking:

Innovation often arises from taking risks, challenging the status quo, and embracing uncertainty. AI systems are designed to minimize risks and optimize outcomes based on historical data and patterns. However, this risk aversion may discourage individuals from taking bold and innovative initiatives. If humans become overly reliant on AI for decision-making and idea generation, it may impede the exploration of uncharted territories and limit breakthrough innovations.

4.5. Influence on Artistic Expression:
AI technologies have been used in various artistic domains, such as music composition, visual arts, and film production. While AI-generated art can be intriguing, it raises questions about the role of human creativity and the authenticity of artistic expression. If AI-driven artistic creation becomes predominant, it may reshape the landscape of artistic production and diminish the appreciation for human-generated artistic works.

The Social Impact of AI on Human Intelligence

5.1. Impact on Social Interaction:
AI technologies, such as social media algorithms and chatbots, have transformed the way humans

interact and communicate. While these advancements offer convenience and efficiency, they can also lead to unintended consequences for human intelligence and social interactions. The algorithms used by social media platforms to personalize content and recommendations may create echo chambers, where individuals are exposed only to information that aligns with their existing beliefs and preferences. This can lead to a narrowing of perspectives, limited exposure to diverse opinions, and hinder critical thinking and open dialogue.

5.2. Polarization and Echo Chambers:

AI algorithms that prioritize engagement and maximize user attention may inadvertently contribute to societal polarization. By presenting individuals with content that aligns with their existing views, AI-driven platforms can reinforce biases and create echo chambers. This can further divide societies, hinder constructive dialogue, and impede the development of well-rounded perspectives.

5.3. Dehumanization and Social Inequality:
The integration of AI in various industries, such as customer service and automation, can lead to the dehumanization of social interactions. When individuals primarily interact with AI systems rather than humans, there is a risk of eroding empathy, compassion, and understanding. Moreover, the widespread adoption of AI may exacerbate social inequality if access to AI technologies and the benefits they bring are unequally distributed across socioeconomic groups.

5.4. The Erosion of Trust:
Trust is a vital component of social interactions, and AI can have a profound impact on trust dynamics. If AI systems are perceived as biased, unaccountable, or unreliable, it can erode trust in institutions and technological advancements. Concerns about AI ethics, transparency, and the

potential for manipulation can lead to skepticism and a breakdown of trust between individuals and AI-driven systems.

5.5. Implications for Employment and Labor Market:

The automation potential of AI has raised concerns about job displacement and the future of work. As AI systems become increasingly capable of performing complex tasks, there is a risk of significant job losses in various industries. This can have detrimental effects on individuals' livelihoods, economic stability, and overall well-being. Furthermore, the need for upskilling and reskilling to adapt to the changing job landscape poses challenges for society at large.

Ethical Considerations in AI Development

6.1. Algorithmic Bias:

AI systems are only as unbiased as the data they are trained on. If the training data is biased, it can lead to algorithmic bias, perpetuating societal inequalities and discrimination. Bias in AI can manifest in various ways, such as racial profiling in facial recognition systems or gender bias in hiring algorithms. Addressing algorithmic bias is crucial to ensure fairness and equity in AI systems.

6.2. Privacy and Data Security Concerns:

AI technologies rely on vast amounts of data for training and decision-making. This raises concerns about data privacy and security. The collection, storage, and utilization of personal data by AI systems can infringe upon individuals' privacy rights. Robust measures and regulations are necessary to protect personal data and prevent its misuse or unauthorized access.

6.3. Autonomous Decision-Making and Accountability:

As AI systems become more autonomous, there is a pressing need to address issues of accountability and responsibility. When AI systems make decisions with significant societal implications, such as autonomous vehicles or healthcare diagnosis, it becomes crucial to establish mechanisms for oversight, transparency, and accountability. Ensuring that humans can understand and explain AI decisions is essential for building trust and addressing potential ethical dilemmas.

6.4. Human Rights Implications:
The deployment of AI technologies can have profound implications for human rights. Facial recognition, surveillance systems, and predictive policing algorithms raise concerns about privacy, freedom of expression, and the right to a fair trial. It is essential to carefully evaluate and regulate the use of AI to safeguard human rights and prevent the misuse of technology for surveillance and control.

6.5. Exploitation and Misuse of AI:
AI technologies can be vulnerable to exploitation and misuse for various malicious purposes. Malicious actors can use AI to spread

misinformation, launch cyber attacks, or manipulate public opinion. Deep Fakes, for example, can be used to create highly realistic yet fabricated videos that can deceive and manipulate individuals. Safeguarding AI systems against misuse and developing robust security measures are critical to mitigate these risks.

Mitigating the Negative Impact of AI on Human Intelligence

7.1. Education and Adaptability:
Education plays a pivotal role in preparing individuals for the AI-driven future. Emphasizing critical thinking, problem-solving, creativity, and emotional intelligence in educational curricula can help individuals develop skills that complement AI technologies. Lifelong learning and adaptability should be encouraged to ensure individuals can thrive in a rapidly evolving technological landscape.

7.2. Ethical AI Development:

Ethics should be at the core of AI development and deployment. Organizations and developers must prioritize ethical considerations and ensure transparency, accountability, and fairness in AI systems. Comprehensive guidelines, standards, and regulatory frameworks should be established to govern AI development, address algorithmic bias, and safeguard human values and rights.

7.3. Human-AI Collaboration:
Promoting collaboration between humans and AI systems can harness the strengths of both. AI can assist humans in complex decision-making processes, augmenting human intelligence rather than replacing it. Designing AI systems that empower individuals, provide explanations, and encourage human oversight can help mitigate the negative impact on human intelligence.

7.4. Enhancing Emotional and Creative Skills:
To counterbalance the potential negative impact of AI on emotional intelligence and creativity,

individuals should actively cultivate and enhance these skills. Emphasizing emotional awareness, empathy, and fostering opportunities for creative expression can help maintain and develop these essential aspects of human intelligence.

7.5. Regulation and Policy-making:
Governments and policymakers play a crucial role in shaping the development and deployment of AI. Robust regulations and policies are necessary to ensure ethical AI practices, protect individuals' rights, and address the potential negative impact on human intelligence. Collaboration between policymakers, industry experts, and researchers is essential to strike a balance between technological advancements and societal well-being.

While AI presents significant opportunities for enhancing various aspects of human life, it is crucial to recognize and address the potential negative impact on human intelligence. The cognitive, emotional, creativity, and social dimensions of human intelligence can be affected by overreliance on AI, algorithmic bias, and ethical concerns. By understanding these potential risks and taking proactive measures, such as promoting ethical AI development, fostering human-AI collaboration, and enhancing emotional and creative skills, we can mitigate the negative impact and ensure responsible and beneficial integration of AI into our society. It is imperative to prioritize the well-being and development of human intelligence while harnessing the transformative potential of AI.

Introduction to Understanding Human Intelligence

Human intelligence is a complex and fascinating aspect of our existence. It is the ability to acquire knowledge, apply reasoning, solve problems, adapt to new situations, and exhibit creativity. From the earliest civilizations to the modern era, humans have been intrigued by the workings of their own minds and have strived to understand the nature and mechanisms of intelligence.

In this extensive exploration of human intelligence, we will delve into various aspects of its understanding. We will discuss the historical perspectives, theoretical frameworks, cognitive processes, factors influencing intelligence, and advancements in research and technology that contribute to our understanding of this remarkable human trait.

Historical Perspectives on Intelligence:

The study of intelligence has a long and diverse history. Ancient civilizations, such as the Greeks and the Chinese, contemplated the nature of intelligence. However, it was in the late 19th and early 20th centuries that systematic investigations into intelligence began. We will explore the contributions of influential psychologists and philosophers like Alfred Binet, Charles Spearman, Howard Gardner, and others who shaped the field of intelligence research.

Defining Intelligence:

Defining intelligence has been a challenging task throughout history. Different perspectives have emerged, ranging from the general notion of a single underlying factor (g-factor) to multiple intelligences encompassing diverse abilities. We will examine the various definitions and theories of intelligence, including psychometric theories, cognitive theories, and cultural perspectives.

Cognitive Processes and Intelligence:

To understand intelligence, it is essential to explore the cognitive processes that underlie intelligent behavior. We will discuss key cognitive functions such as perception, attention, memory, language, problem-solving, decision-making, and creativity. By examining these processes, we can gain insights into how they contribute to the manifestation of intelligence in different domains.

The Nature-Nurture Debate:

One of the longstanding debates in understanding human intelligence is the nature-nurture debate. Are intelligence and cognitive abilities primarily determined by genetics (nature) or influenced by environmental factors (nurture)? We will delve into the research on genetic and environmental influences on intelligence, including studies on heritability, gene-environment interactions, and the role of education and socioeconomic factors.

Emotional Intelligence:

While traditional notions of intelligence focused on cognitive abilities, the concept of emotional intelligence introduced a new dimension to our understanding of human intelligence. Emotional intelligence refers to the ability to recognize, understand, manage, and express emotions, both in oneself and others. We will explore the components of emotional intelligence and its significance in personal and social interactions.

Intelligence Testing:
Intelligence tests have played a crucial role in assessing and measuring intelligence. We will explore the development of intelligence tests, including the Stanford-Binet Intelligence Scales, Wechsler Adult Intelligence Scale (WAIS), and Raven's Progressive Matrices. We will also discuss the limitations and controversies surrounding intelligence testing, such as cultural biases and the concept of multiple intelligences.

Intellectual Disability and Giftedness:

While intelligence is distributed across a wide spectrum, some individuals face challenges due to intellectual disabilities, whereas others exhibit exceptional intellectual abilities and giftedness. We will examine the definitions, characteristics, and assessment of intellectual disability and giftedness. Furthermore, we will explore the implications of these conditions on education, support systems, and society at large.

Neuroscience and Intelligence:
Advancements in neuroscience have significantly contributed to our understanding of human intelligence. Brain imaging techniques, such as functional magnetic resonance imaging (fMRI) and electroencephalography (EEG), have allowed researchers to study brain activity associated with intelligence. We will delve into the neuroscience of intelligence, examining brain regions, neural networks, and neurochemical processes implicated in intelligent behavior.

Artificial Intelligence and Human Intelligence:

The rise of artificial intelligence (AI) has sparked debates and comparisons between machine intelligence and human intelligence. We will explore the intersection of AI and human intelligence, discussing areas where AI has surpassed human capabilities, such as chess-playing programs and language translation algorithms. Additionally, we will examine the unique qualities of human intelligence that are challenging to replicate in machines, such as creativity, intuition, and ethical decision-making.

Cultural and Social Perspectives on Intelligence:

Intelligence is influenced by cultural and social factors. Different cultures value and define intelligence in distinct ways. We will explore cultural variations in intelligence, including the concept of cultural intelligence and how cultural beliefs and practices shape cognitive abilities. Moreover, we will examine the impact of socioeconomic factors, education, and social environments on intelligence and cognitive development.

Developmental Perspectives:
Understanding intelligence requires studying its development across the lifespan. We will explore cognitive development theories, such as Jean Piaget's stages of cognitive development, and examine how intelligence evolves from infancy to old age. We will discuss the influence of genetics, environment, and social interactions on cognitive development and explore factors that promote intellectual growth and potential.

Creativity and Intelligence:
Creativity is closely intertwined with intelligence. We will explore the relationship between creativity and intelligence, examining different theories and perspectives on creative thinking and problem-solving. We will also discuss the role of divergent thinking, domain-specific expertise, and environmental factors in fostering creativity and its

impact on various domains, including arts, sciences, and entrepreneurship.

Enhancing and Developing Intelligence:
Can intelligence be enhanced or developed? We will explore the concept of cognitive enhancement, including educational interventions, brain-training programs, and neurofeedback techniques that aim to improve cognitive abilities. We will also discuss the ethics and implications of cognitive enhancement and the importance of considering individual differences and diverse learning styles.

The Future of Intelligence Research:
As our understanding of human intelligence evolves, we are likely to witness exciting advancements in intelligence research. We will explore emerging trends and future directions in the field, such as the integration of neuroscience and artificial intelligence, the study of collective intelligence and networked systems, and the exploration of cognitive enhancements through

technology. We will also discuss the ethical considerations and potential societal impacts of these advancements.

Understanding human intelligence is a multidimensional and ever-evolving endeavor. From historical perspectives to cutting-edge research, this comprehensive exploration has provided insights into the nature, cognitive processes, cultural influences, and future directions of intelligence research. As we continue to unravel the mysteries of human intelligence, we gain a deeper appreciation for the remarkable capabilities of the human mind and the potential it holds for shaping our world.

Definition of Human Intelligence

Human intelligence is a complex and multifaceted concept that has been the subject of study and speculation for centuries. It encompasses various cognitive abilities, including reasoning, problem-solving, learning, memory, creativity, and the capacity for emotional and social understanding. Defining human intelligence has been a challenging task for researchers, philosophers, and psychologists alike. In this extensive exploration, we will delve into the definition of human intelligence, examining different perspectives and theories that have emerged over time.

Historical Perspectives on Human Intelligence:

1.1 Ancient Views:

Ancient civilizations, such as the Greeks and Egyptians, held diverse beliefs about intelligence.

Plato's concept of intelligence: The "rational soul" that governs a person's thoughts and actions.

Aristotle's view: Intellect as the highest form of human capacity.

1.2 Intelligence in the Middle Ages:

Intelligence was associated with divine intervention and was considered an innate quality.

St. Thomas Aquinas and his concept of "agent intellect."

1.3 The Renaissance and Enlightenment:

The shift from theological to more secular perspectives on intelligence.

René Descartes and the distinction between mind and body.

John Locke's notion of tabula rasa and the importance of experience in shaping intelligence.

Psychometric Approaches to Intelligence:

2.1 Early Psychometric Tests:

Francis Galton and the development of the first intelligence tests.

Alfred Binet and the creation of the first modern intelligence test.

2.2 Theories of General Intelligence:

Charles Spearman's concept of a general intelligence factor (g).

Louis Thurstone's multiple intelligence theory.

Raymond Cattell's fluid and crystallized intelligence.

2.3 Contemporary Intelligence Tests:

The Stanford-Binet Intelligence Scales.

Wechsler Adult Intelligence Scale (WAIS).

Limitations and criticisms of intelligence testing.

Cognitive Approaches to Intelligence:

3.1 Information Processing Theory:

The mind as an information processor.

The cognitive processes underlying intelligence, such as attention, perception, memory, and problem-solving.

3.2 Theory of Multiple Intelligences:

Howard Gardner's theory of multiple intelligences.
Linguistic, logical-mathematical, spatial, musical, bodily-kinesthetic, interpersonal, intrapersonal, and naturalistic intelligences.

3.3 Emotional Intelligence:

Peter Salovey and John Mayer's initial concept of emotional intelligence.
Daniel Goleman's popularization and expansion of the concept.
Components of emotional intelligence: self-awareness, self-regulation, motivation, empathy, and social skills.
Neuroscientific Perspectives on Intelligence:
4.1 Brain Structure and Intelligence:

Studies exploring the relationship between brain structure and intelligence.

The role of frontal and parietal lobes, hippocampus, and other brain regions in intelligence.

4.2 Neural Networks and Intelligence:

Connectionist models and their implications for understanding intelligence.

The importance of neural networks and synaptic plasticity in learning and intelligence.

Cultural and Contextual Influences on Intelligence:

5.1 Cultural Perspectives on Intelligence:

The impact of culture on the definition and measurement of intelligence.

Cross-cultural variations in intelligence tests and performance.

5.2 Socioeconomic Factors:

The influence of socioeconomic status on intelligence.

The Flynn effect and rising IQ scores over time.

Artificial Intelligence and Human Intelligence:

6.1 AI vs. Human Intelligence:

Comparisons between artificial intelligence and human intelligence.

The capabilities and limitations of AI systems.

6.2 Human-AI Collaboration:

The potential for human-AI collaboration and synergy.

Ethical considerations and challenges of integrating AI and human intelligence.

Cognitive Abilities and Skills: Unleashing the Power of the Human Mind

Human cognitive abilities and skills are at the core of our intelligence and define our capacity to understand, process, and utilize information. These cognitive abilities encompass a wide range of mental processes, including perception, attention, memory, language, problem-solving, reasoning, and decision-making. Our cognitive skills play a crucial role in shaping our thoughts, actions, and overall performance in various domains of life, from education and work to personal relationships and creative endeavors. This article explores the fascinating realm of human cognitive abilities and skills, shedding light on their nature, development, and potential for growth.

Perception:
Perception forms the foundation of our cognitive processes, enabling us to make sense of the world

around us. It involves the interpretation of sensory information received through our senses—sight, hearing, touch, taste, and smell. The human brain effortlessly integrates these sensory inputs, constructing our conscious experience of reality. Perception is a complex interplay between bottom-up processing (data-driven) and top-down processing (conceptually driven). Factors such as attention, context, and previous experiences influence our perception, highlighting the subjectivity of our sensory experiences.

Attention:
Attention is the cognitive ability to selectively focus on specific stimuli or information while filtering out irrelevant or distracting inputs. It plays a crucial role in learning, memory, problem-solving, and decision-making. Attention can be divided into various forms, such as sustained attention (maintaining focus over time), selective attention (focusing on a specific stimulus), divided attention (processing multiple stimuli simultaneously), and

executive attention (managing attentional resources). Attentional control can be trained and improved through practice and strategies like mindfulness.

Memory:
Memory encompasses the processes involved in acquiring, storing, and retrieving information. It is essential for learning, problem-solving, and everyday functioning. Memory can be divided into three main types: sensory memory (brief storage of sensory information), short-term memory (temporary storage of information), and long-term memory (relatively permanent storage). Within long-term memory, there are further subdivisions, including episodic memory (personal experiences), semantic memory (general knowledge), and procedural memory (skills and procedures). Techniques like mnemonic devices and spaced repetition can enhance memory performance.

Language:

Language is a unique cognitive ability that sets humans apart from other species. It allows us to communicate, express thoughts and emotions, convey information, and engage in social interactions. Language involves several interconnected components, including phonology (sounds), morphology (word structure), syntax (sentence structure), semantics (meaning), and pragmatics (language use in context). Language acquisition occurs naturally during childhood through exposure to linguistic input, but it can also be learned and refined throughout life.

Problem-Solving and Reasoning:
Problem-solving and reasoning are fundamental cognitive skills that involve analyzing information, identifying patterns, generating solutions, and making logical deductions. These skills are vital across various domains, including mathematics, science, technology, and everyday life. Problem-solving can be approached through different strategies, such as trial and error,

algorithms, heuristics, and insight. Reasoning encompasses deductive reasoning (drawing logical conclusions from general principles) and inductive reasoning (drawing generalizations based on specific observations).

Decision-Making:
Decision-making refers to the cognitive process of selecting a course of action from among several alternatives. It involves evaluating options, considering potential outcomes and risks, and choosing the best option based on personal goals and values. Decision-making can be influenced by cognitive biases, emotions, and external factors. Developing decision-making skills involves improving information processing, critical thinking, and considering diverse perspectives.

Creativity:
Creativity is a cognitive ability that enables us to generate original and valuable ideas, solutions, and artistic expressions.

Creativity involves divergent thinking, the ability to generate multiple ideas and explore different perspectives. It also requires convergent thinking, the ability to evaluate and select the most promising ideas. Creative thinking is characterized by flexibility, originality, fluency, and elaboration. It can be enhanced through techniques such as brainstorming, mind mapping, and exposure to diverse experiences and stimuli. Creativity is not limited to artistic pursuits but is relevant in problem-solving, innovation, and all areas of human endeavor.

Cognitive Flexibility:
Cognitive flexibility refers to the ability to adapt and switch between different cognitive processes or mental frameworks to meet changing demands. It involves shifting attention, adjusting strategies, and considering alternative perspectives. Cognitive flexibility is crucial for problem-solving, learning, creativity, and effective decision-making. It can be developed through activities that promote

perspective-taking, exposure to diverse viewpoints, and engaging in tasks that require mental agility.

Metacognition:
Metacognition is the awareness and understanding of one's own cognitive processes. It involves monitoring and regulating one's thinking, learning, and problem-solving strategies. Metacognitive skills allow individuals to reflect on their knowledge, evaluate their understanding, and make adjustments to optimize their learning and performance. Metacognition plays a vital role in self-directed learning, critical thinking, and lifelong intellectual growth.

Cognitive Development:
Cognitive abilities and skills undergo significant development throughout life, with notable milestones occurring during childhood and adolescence. Jean Piaget's theory of cognitive development posits that children progress through distinct stages, including the sensorimotor stage

(0-2 years), preoperational stage (2-7 years), concrete operational stage (7-11 years), and formal operational stage (11+ years). Each stage is characterized by different cognitive capacities, such as object permanence, conservation, abstract reasoning, and hypothetical thinking. However, cognitive development is not limited to childhood, as learning and cognitive abilities continue to evolve and adapt in response to new experiences and challenges.

Factors Influencing Cognitive Abilities:
Various factors influence the development and expression of cognitive abilities and skills. Genetic factors contribute to individual differences in cognitive functioning, determining the baseline capacity for intellectual abilities. Environmental factors, such as early experiences, education, socioeconomic status, and cultural influences, also shape cognitive development. Additionally, lifestyle factors like nutrition, physical exercise, and sleep have a significant impact on cognitive performance.

Mental health conditions, neurological disorders, and aging can also affect cognitive abilities.

Enhancing Cognitive Abilities:
While cognitive abilities have a biological basis, they are not fixed and can be enhanced through deliberate effort and targeted interventions. Neuroplasticity, the brain's ability to reorganize and form new connections, enables the development and refinement of cognitive skills. Engaging in intellectually stimulating activities, such as reading, puzzles, and learning new skills, promotes cognitive growth. Regular exercise, healthy nutrition, stress management, and adequate sleep also support optimal cognitive functioning. Furthermore, educational strategies and interventions can be designed to cultivate specific cognitive abilities in individuals.

Cognitive Abilities and the Digital Age:
The advent of technology and the digital age have significantly influenced cognitive abilities and

skills. While technology offers new opportunities for learning, communication, and problem-solving, it also poses challenges. The constant exposure to digital stimuli, multitasking, and information overload can impact attention, memory, and critical thinking. Digital literacy, including the ability to navigate and evaluate online information, has become an essential cognitive skill in the modern era.

The Future of Cognitive Abilities:
As our understanding of the human brain and cognitive processes continues to advance, so does our potential to enhance and utilize our cognitive abilities. Emerging fields such as neurofeedback, cognitive training programs, and brain-computer interfaces hold promise for optimizing cognitive performance.

Artificial intelligence
The Future of Cognitive Abilities (continued):

(AI) and machine learning technologies are also shaping the landscape of cognitive abilities, with developments in areas such as natural language processing and pattern recognition. These advancements open up possibilities for augmenting human cognition, such as improving memory, decision-making, and problem-solving through the integration of human and artificial intelligence.

However, as we explore the frontiers of cognitive enhancement, ethical considerations arise. Questions about privacy, autonomy, and equity must be addressed to ensure that cognitive technologies are developed and implemented responsibly. Additionally, the potential impact of cognitive enhancements on social dynamics and the notion of what it means to be human necessitates ongoing dialogue and ethical deliberation.

Human cognitive abilities and skills are the cornerstone of our intelligence and shape our understanding of the world, our interactions with others, and our capacity to solve problems and create new ideas. Perception, attention, memory, language, problem-solving, reasoning, decision-making, and creativity are among the key cognitive abilities that contribute to our intellectual prowess.

Understanding the nature of these abilities, their development, and their potential for growth allows us to harness the power of the human mind to its fullest extent. Through intentional practice, education, and the integration of new technologies, we can enhance our cognitive abilities and unlock our intellectual potential.

As we navigate the challenges and opportunities of the digital age and explore the frontiers of cognitive enhancement, it is crucial to approach these advancements with a thoughtful and ethical mindset. Balancing innovation with considerations of privacy, autonomy, and equity will be essential in ensuring that cognitive technologies are developed and implemented responsibly, benefiting individuals and society as a whole.

Ultimately, our cognitive abilities and skills are not only a testament to the remarkable capabilities of the human brain but also an invitation to continuously explore and expand the boundaries of our intellectual capabilities, both individually and collectively.

Importance of Human Intelligence in Problem Solving and Decision Making

In the realm of problem solving and decision making, human intelligence plays a vital role. While the advent of technology and artificial intelligence has revolutionized several domains, the unique capabilities of human intelligence remain unparalleled. This essay explores the importance of human intelligence in problem solving and decision making, highlighting its distinct characteristics, cognitive abilities, and emotional intelligence. By understanding the significance of human intelligence, we can better appreciate the complexities involved in addressing complex challenges and making effective decisions in various aspects of life.

The Distinct Characteristics of Human Intelligence: Human intelligence encompasses a range of distinct characteristics that contribute to problem solving and decision making. One crucial aspect is our capacity for critical thinking, which enables us to analyze information, assess its validity, and draw logical conclusions. Critical thinking involves evaluating evidence, recognizing biases, and employing reasoning skills to solve problems effectively.

Another vital characteristic is creativity. Human intelligence allows us to think outside the box, generate innovative ideas, and devise novel solutions to complex problems. Creativity fosters adaptability and flexibility, enabling us to adapt our problem-solving approaches based on changing circumstances.

Furthermore, human intelligence is intertwined with intuition. Intuition refers to our ability to make rapid decisions based on our gut feelings and previous experiences. It complements rational thinking and helps us navigate uncertain situations when time is limited and the available information is incomplete.

Cognitive Abilities in Problem Solving and Decision Making:
Human intelligence encompasses various cognitive abilities that facilitate problem solving and decision making. These abilities include perception, attention, memory, and learning.

Perception allows us to gather information from our environment and interpret it, forming the basis of problem identification and understanding. Attention enables us to focus on relevant details while filtering out distractions, aiding in the identification of critical aspects of a problem.

Memory plays a crucial role in problem solving and decision making by storing past experiences, knowledge, and lessons learned. Retrieving relevant information from memory helps us identify patterns, similarities, and differences, leading to more informed decisions.

Moreover, the process of learning empowers humans to acquire new knowledge and skills, allowing us to adapt and improve our problem-solving capabilities over time. Learning involves reasoning, making connections between different pieces of information, and updating mental models to accommodate new insights.

Emotional Intelligence in Problem Solving and Decision Making:
Human intelligence extends beyond cognitive abilities and encompasses emotional intelligence, which is vital for effective problem solving and decision making. Emotional intelligence involves the ability to perceive, understand, and manage our emotions and the emotions of others.

In problem-solving scenarios, emotional intelligence allows individuals to remain calm and composed, even under high-pressure situations. It helps in controlling impulsive reactions and maintaining a rational and objective mindset, leading to more accurate problem analysis.

Furthermore, emotional intelligence enhances interpersonal skills, enabling effective collaboration and communication among team members involved in problem-solving processes. Empathy, a key component of emotional intelligence, allows individuals to understand and consider the perspectives and emotions of others, fostering cooperation and facilitating consensus-building.

Complex Problem Solving and Decision Making: Human intelligence is particularly crucial in addressing complex problems that require sophisticated analysis and evaluation. Complex problems often involve multiple variables, uncertainties, and interdependencies. Human intelligence allows us to break down complex problems into manageable components, understand the underlying factors, and identify potential solutions.

The ability to engage in critical thinking and employ cognitive flexibility is essential when faced with complex problems. Human intelligence enables us to generate alternative solutions, evaluate their potential outcomes, and select the most suitable course of action based on a holistic assessment of the situation.

Moreover, human intelligence excels in situations where ethical considerations and moral judgments are paramount. The capacity for moral reasoning allows individuals to evaluate the consequences of their decisions and consider the ethical implications of various courses of action. This consideration of ethics and values is crucial in problem solving and decision making, as it ensures that the chosen solutions align with societal norms and promote the well-being of individuals and communities.

Contextual Understanding and Judgment:
Human intelligence is invaluable in problem solving and decision making because it incorporates contextual understanding and judgment. Unlike artificial intelligence systems that rely on predefined rules and algorithms, human intelligence takes into account the unique circumstances, cultural nuances, and social dynamics of a given situation.

Contextual understanding allows individuals to evaluate problems in their entirety, considering the various factors and relationships at play. This holistic perspective enables the identification of underlying causes, potential constraints, and unintended consequences of different solutions. By incorporating contextual understanding, human intelligence mitigates the risk of implementing shortsighted or one-size-fits-all solutions.

Additionally, human intelligence excels in situations where judgments need to be made based on incomplete or ambiguous information. Through their ability to reason and weigh different possibilities, individuals can make informed decisions, even in uncertain environments. Human intelligence acknowledges the limitations of available information and employs cognitive processes to assess risks, uncertainties, and trade-offs.

Ethical Considerations and Value-Based Decision Making:
Problem solving and decision making are not merely about finding the most efficient or optimal solution. Human intelligence brings ethical considerations and value-based decision making to the forefront. Humans possess a moral compass and the capacity for empathy, enabling them to evaluate the impact of their decisions on individuals, communities, and the environment.

Value-based decision making takes into account personal values, societal norms, and long-term consequences. It involves considering the ethical implications, sustainability, and social responsibility of different choices. Human intelligence ensures that decisions align with our fundamental principles and contribute to the greater good.

Furthermore, human intelligence is essential in navigating ethical dilemmas that may arise in problem-solving processes. These dilemmas often involve conflicting values or competing interests, and human intelligence enables individuals to carefully balance and prioritize different considerations. It allows for a nuanced evaluation of potential risks and benefits, facilitating ethical decision making in complex scenarios.

The Human Element in Collaboration and Leadership:
Problem solving and decision making are rarely solitary endeavors. They often require collaboration and leadership, where human intelligence plays a

pivotal role. Human intelligence facilitates effective communication, active listening, and empathy, fostering productive teamwork and collective problem-solving efforts.

In collaborative settings, individuals can leverage their diverse perspectives, knowledge, and experiences to approach problems from multiple angles. The collective intelligence generated through collaboration often leads to more comprehensive problem analysis and innovative solutions that may not have been identified by a single individual.

Leadership is another domain where human intelligence is indispensable. Effective leaders possess a deep understanding of human behavior, motivation, and emotions. They are skilled in empowering and motivating team members, encouraging creativity, and facilitating decision-making processes. Leadership requires emotional intelligence, strategic thinking, and the ability to inspire and influence others, which are unique capabilities of human intelligence.

The Future of Human Intelligence in Problem Solving and Decision Making:
As technology continues to advance and artificial intelligence becomes more sophisticated, the role of human intelligence in problem solving and decision making may undergo transformation. Automation and AI systems can undoubtedly assist in data analysis, pattern recognition, and decision support. However, human intelligence remains vital in several critical aspects.

Human intelligence brings the human touch, creativity, and contextual understanding that are difficult to replicate in machines. It provides the capacity to consider ethical implications, manage complex social dynamics, and navigate uncertain and ambiguous situations. Moreover, human intelligence fosters emotional connections, empathy, and trust, which are crucial in collaborative problem solving and decision making.

The future lies in harnessing the synergy between human intelligence and artificial intelligence. Integrating the strengths of both can lead to powerful problem-solving and decision-making processes. Human intelligence can guide AI systems by providing ethical guidelines, ensuring fairness, and overseeing the implementation of decisions. AI, on the other hand, can enhance human intelligence by processing vast amounts of data, identifying patterns, and generating insights that may not be immediately apparent to humans.

In this collaborative relationship, humans can leverage AI as a tool to augment their problem-solving and decision-making capabilities. AI systems can assist in data analysis, simulations, and scenario modeling, providing valuable insights and recommendations. However, the final decision-making authority and responsibility still rest with human intelligence, considering the ethical, social, and contextual factors that AI may not fully comprehend.

It is crucial to recognize that while AI can automate certain aspects of problem solving and decision making, it does not possess human-like consciousness, intuition, or the ability to understand complex emotions. These uniquely human qualities remain essential in addressing complex challenges that require empathy, creativity, and moral reasoning.

Human intelligence plays a fundamental role in problem solving and decision making. Its distinct characteristics, cognitive abilities, emotional intelligence, and value-based judgment contribute to effective problem analysis, innovative solutions, and ethical decision making. Human intelligence excels in complex and ambiguous situations, incorporating contextual understanding, considering multiple perspectives, and balancing competing interests.

While AI and technology have their place in supporting problem-solving processes, they cannot replicate the breadth and depth of human intelligence. Human intelligence brings creativity, critical thinking, ethical considerations, and the human element of collaboration and leadership. It allows for adaptive thinking, holistic evaluation, and the ability to navigate uncertainty and ambiguity.

As we move forward in the era of advancing technology, it is crucial to embrace the potential synergy between human intelligence and AI. By leveraging the strengths of both, we can harness the power of data-driven insights while maintaining the uniquely human qualities that are indispensable in problem solving and decision making.

In a world that is becoming increasingly complex and interconnected, the importance of human intelligence in problem solving and decision making cannot be overstated. It is through the integration of cognitive abilities, emotional intelligence, ethical considerations, and collaboration that we can address the challenges of our time and shape a better future for humanity.

3.1 Definition and Types of Artificial Intelligence

Artificial Intelligence (AI) is a branch of computer science that focuses on creating intelligent machines that can perform tasks that would typically require human intelligence. These tasks include speech recognition, problem-solving, learning, planning, perception, and decision-making. AI systems aim to mimic human cognitive abilities and provide solutions to complex problems.

Over the years, AI has evolved and encompassed various subfields and approaches. Here, we will explore the different types of AI based on their capabilities and functionalities.

3.1.1 Narrow AI

Narrow AI, also known as weak AI, refers to AI systems designed to perform specific tasks within a limited domain. These systems excel in performing a single task but lack the ability to generalize or transfer their knowledge to other domains. Examples of narrow AI include voice assistants like Amazon's Alexa, recommendation systems, and image recognition algorithms.

Narrow AI operates based on predefined rules or algorithms and requires a significant amount of human involvement for training and supervision. While narrow AI has demonstrated impressive performance in specialized areas, it does not possess true human-like intelligence.

3.1.2 General AI

General AI, also known as strong AI or human-level AI, refers to AI systems that possess the ability to understand, learn, and apply knowledge across various domains. Unlike narrow AI, general AI can handle unfamiliar tasks and adapt its behavior accordingly, similar to human intelligence. General AI aims to replicate human cognitive abilities, including reasoning, problem-solving, and even emotions.

The development of general AI is a significant challenge in the field of AI research. It requires creating machines that can understand the world in a similar way to humans, process vast amounts of information, and exhibit complex decision-making capabilities. Achieving general AI would have profound implications for society, as it could potentially outperform humans in numerous domains.

3.1.3 Superintelligent AI

Superintelligent AI, also referred to as artificial general superintelligence (AGI), represents AI systems that surpass human intelligence across all domains. Superintelligent AI would possess not only cognitive abilities but also the capacity to understand, learn, and improve itself exponentially, leading to rapid advances in knowledge and problem-solving capabilities.

While superintelligent AI remains a hypothetical concept, it has garnered significant attention due to its potential impact on society and the potential risks associated with its development. Experts like Elon Musk and Stephen Hawking have expressed concerns about the risks of uncontrolled superintelligent AI and the need for careful research and regulation.

3.1.4 Machine Learning

Machine Learning (ML) is a subset of AI that focuses on developing algorithms and models that enable systems to learn from data and improve their performance without explicit programming. ML algorithms can analyze and identify patterns within vast amounts of data, allowing systems to make predictions, classifications, and decisions based on the learned patterns.

There are three primary types of machine learning:

3.1.4.1 Supervised Learning

Supervised learning involves training a model on labeled data, where each data instance is associated with a known output or target value. The model learns to make predictions by mapping input data to the corresponding output based on the provided examples. For instance, a supervised learning model can be trained to classify emails as spam or non-spam based on labeled email data.

3.1.4.2 Unsupervised Learning

Unsupervised learning involves training a model on unlabeled data, where the model aims to discover underlying patterns, structures, or relationships within the data. Unlike supervised learning, there are no predefined outputs to guide the learning process. Clustering and dimensionality reduction are common tasks performed using unsupervised learning techniques.

3.1.4.3 Reinforcement Learning

Reinforcement learning involves training an agent to interact with an environment and learn optimal actions through trial and error. The agent receives feedback in the form of rewards or penalties based on its actions, which helps it learn to maximize its cumulative reward over time. Reinforcement learning has been successful in training AI systems to play complex games, control robotic systems, and optimize resource allocation.

3.1.5 Deep Learning

Deep Learning is a subfield of machine learning that focuses on training artificial neural networks with multiple layers (hence the term "deep") to learn hierarchical representations of data. Deep learning models, also known as deep neural networks, are designed to automatically extract relevant features from raw data, enabling them to achieve state-of-the-art performance in various domains such as computer vision, natural language processing, and speech recognition.

Deep learning models are characterized by their architecture, which consists of input layers, hidden layers, and output layers. Each layer contains multiple interconnected nodes, called neurons, which perform computations and pass information to the next layer. Deep learning models learn to adjust the weights and biases of these connections through a process known as backpropagation, where errors are propagated backward through the network to update the parameters and improve the model's performance.

The availability of large datasets, powerful hardware (such as graphics processing units or

GPUs), and advancements in algorithms have fueled the rapid progress of deep learning in recent years. Deep learning has revolutionized areas such as image and speech recognition, natural language understanding, and autonomous driving, leading to significant breakthroughs in AI applications.

3.1.6 Expert Systems

Expert Systems, also known as knowledge-based systems, are AI systems designed to mimic the problem-solving and decision-making abilities of human experts in specific domains. These systems are built on a knowledge base that contains expert knowledge and rules, which are used to reason and provide solutions to complex problems.

Expert systems rely on logical inference and pattern matching to analyze input data and apply the relevant knowledge to generate recommendations or make decisions. They are particularly useful in domains where human expertise is crucial, such as medical diagnosis, financial analysis, and troubleshooting complex systems.

While expert systems have been successful in certain domains, they are limited by their reliance on explicit knowledge representation and the challenges of capturing and maintaining expert knowledge. The development of expert systems often requires extensive collaboration between domain experts and AI researchers to ensure the accuracy and effectiveness of the system.

3.1.7 Natural Language Processing

Natural Language Processing (NLP) is a branch of AI that focuses on enabling computers to understand, interpret, and generate human language. NLP encompasses a wide range of tasks, including speech recognition, sentiment analysis, language translation, and text generation.

NLP systems utilize techniques from machine learning, deep learning, and linguistics to process and analyze natural language data. These systems aim to extract meaning from text or speech, understand context and intent, and generate human-like responses. NLP has found applications in various fields, such as virtual assistants, chatbots, language translation services, and information retrieval systems.

Advancements in deep learning, particularly the development of transformer models like GPT (Generative Pre-trained Transformer), have significantly improved the capabilities of NLP systems. These models can generate coherent and contextually relevant text, leading to more natural and engaging human-computer interactions.

3.1.8 Computer Vision

Computer Vision is a field of AI that focuses on enabling computers to interpret and understand visual information from images or videos. Computer vision algorithms aim to mimic human visual perception by extracting features, recognizing objects, and understanding the spatial relationships within visual data.

Computer vision has numerous applications, including image recognition, object detection and tracking, facial recognition, and scene understanding. It plays a vital role in various domains, such as autonomous vehicles, surveillance systems, medical imaging, and augmented reality.

Deep learning has revolutionized computer vision by enabling the development of deep neural networks, such as convolution neural networks (CNNs), which have achieved remarkable performance in image classification and object detection tasks. CNNs learn to extract hierarchical features from images, allowing them to recognize patterns and objects with high accuracy.

In recent years, computer vision has seen significant advancements in areas such as image segmentation, where algorithms can accurately identify and classify different regions within an image, and image generation, where generative models can create realistic and novel images based on training data. These advancements have paved the way for applications like autonomous driving, medical diagnostics, and visual content creation.

3.1.9 Robotics and Automation

AI has also played a crucial role in the advancement of robotics and automation. Robotic systems integrated with AI technologies can perceive their environment, make decisions, and perform physical tasks with precision and adaptability. These systems are used in various industries, including manufacturing, healthcare, agriculture, and logistics.

AI-powered robots often utilize computer vision, machine learning, and sensor technologies to navigate and interact with their surroundings. They can handle complex tasks such as object manipulation, grasping, and even decision-making in dynamic and unstructured environments. Robotic systems have the potential to increase efficiency, productivity, and safety in many industries, leading to the rise of smart factories, automated warehouses, and robotic-assisted surgeries.

3.1.10 Ethical and Responsible AI

As AI technologies continue to advance, ethical considerations and responsible practices become increasingly important. The rise of AI brings forth various challenges and concerns that need to be addressed to ensure the responsible and beneficial use of these technologies.

One significant ethical concern is the potential impact of AI on jobs and the workforce. Automation and AI-driven systems have the potential to replace certain job roles, leading to unemployment and economic disparities. It is crucial to focus on strategies for retraining and upskilling the workforce to adapt to the changing job landscape brought about by AI.

Another ethical consideration is the potential bias in AI systems. Machine learning models are trained on datasets that may contain inherent biases, leading to discriminatory outcomes. It is important to ensure that AI systems are trained on diverse and representative datasets and that algorithms are regularly audited to mitigate bias and ensure fairness and equity.

Privacy and data protection are also significant concerns in the age of AI. AI systems often rely on vast amounts of personal data to learn and make predictions. It is essential to establish robust data governance frameworks to protect individuals' privacy and ensure the responsible handling and storage of data.

Transparency and explainability are crucial for building trust in AI systems. As AI technologies become more complex and powerful, it becomes challenging to understand how decisions are made. Efforts are being made to develop methods and techniques that allow AI systems to provide explanations for their decisions and actions, enabling users to understand and verify the reasoning behind the system's outputs.

Finally, the safety and security of AI systems are paramount. As AI technologies become more autonomous and capable, ensuring their reliability and robustness becomes crucial. Steps need to be taken to prevent malicious use of AI and to develop mechanisms that guarantee the safety and security of AI systems in critical domains like healthcare, transportation, and defense.

To address these ethical concerns, policymakers, researchers, and industry leaders must collaborate to establish ethical frameworks, guidelines, and regulations that promote the responsible development, deployment, and use of AI technologies.

The rise of artificial intelligence has brought significant advancements and transformative changes to various fields. From narrow AI systems that excel in specific tasks to the pursuit of general and superintelligent AI, the capabilities of AI technologies continue to expand.

Machine learning, deep learning, expert systems, natural language processing, computer vision, and robotics are some of the key branches and applications of AI. These technologies have demonstrated remarkable achievements in areas such as image recognition, speech synthesis, autonomous driving, and medical diagnosis.

3.1 Definition and Types of Artificial Intelligence

Artificial Intelligence (AI) is a branch of computer science that focuses on creating intelligent machines that can perform tasks that would typically require human intelligence. These tasks include speech recognition, problem-solving, learning, planning, perception, and decision-making. AI systems aim to mimic human cognitive abilities and provide solutions to complex problems.

Over the years, AI has evolved and encompassed various subfields and approaches. Here, we will explore the different types of AI based on their capabilities and functionalities.

3.1.1 Narrow AI

Narrow AI, also known as weak AI, refers to AI systems designed to perform specific tasks within a limited domain. These systems excel in performing a single task but lack the ability to generalize or transfer their knowledge to other domains. Examples of narrow AI include voice assistants like Amazon's Alexa, recommendation systems, and image recognition algorithms.

Narrow AI operates based on predefined rules or algorithms and requires a significant amount of human involvement for training and supervision. While narrow AI has demonstrated impressive performance in specialized areas, it does not possess true human-like intelligence.

3.1.2 General AI

General AI, also known as strong AI or human-level AI, refers to AI systems that possess the ability to understand, learn, and apply knowledge across various domains. Unlike narrow AI, general AI can handle unfamiliar tasks and adapt its behavior accordingly, similar to human intelligence. General AI aims to replicate human cognitive abilities, including reasoning, problem-solving, and even emotions.

The development of general AI is a significant challenge in the field of AI research. It requires creating machines that can understand the world in a similar way to humans, process vast amounts of information, and exhibit complex decision-making capabilities. Achieving general AI would have profound implications for society, as it could potentially outperform humans in numerous domains.

3.1.3 Superintelligent AI

Superintelligent AI, also referred to as artificial general superintelligence (AGI), represents AI systems that surpass human intelligence across all domains. Superintelligent AI would possess not only cognitive abilities but also the capacity to understand, learn, and improve itself exponentially, leading to rapid advances in knowledge and problem-solving capabilities.

While superintelligent AI remains a hypothetical concept, it has garnered significant attention due to its potential impact on society and the potential risks associated with its development. Experts like Elon Musk and Stephen Hawking have expressed concerns about the risks of uncontrolled superintelligent AI and the need for careful research and regulation.

3.1.4 Machine Learning

Machine Learning (ML) is a subset of AI that focuses on developing algorithms and models that enable systems to learn from data and improve their performance without explicit programming. ML algorithms can analyze and identify patterns within vast amounts of data, allowing systems to make predictions, classifications, and decisions based on the learned patterns.

There are three primary types of machine learning:

3.1.4.1 Supervised Learning

Supervised learning involves training a model on labeled data, where each data instance is associated with a known output or target value. The model learns to make predictions by mapping input data to the corresponding output based on the provided examples. For instance, a supervised learning model can be trained to classify emails as spam or non-spam based on labeled email data.

3.1.4.2 Unsupervised Learning

Unsupervised learning involves training a model on unlabeled data, where the model aims to discover underlying patterns, structures, or relationships within the data. Unlike supervised learning, there are no predefined outputs to guide the learning process. Clustering and dimensionality reduction are common tasks performed using unsupervised learning techniques.

3.1.4.3 Reinforcement Learning

Reinforcement learning involves training an agent to interact with an environment and learn optimal actions through trial and error. The agent receives feedback in the form of rewards or penalties based on its actions, which helps it learn to maximize its cumulative reward over time. Reinforcement learning has been successful in training AI systems to play complex games, control robotic systems, and optimize resource allocation.

3.1.5 Deep Learning

Deep Learning is a subfield of machine learning that focuses on training artificial neural networks with multiple layers (hence the term "deep") to learn hierarchical representations of data. Deep learning models, also known as deep neural networks, are designed to automatically extract relevant features from raw data, enabling them to achieve state-of-the-art performance in various domains such as computer vision, natural language processing, and speech recognition.

Deep learning models are characterized by their architecture, which consists of input layers, hidden layers, and output layers. Each layer contains multiple interconnected nodes, called neurons, which perform computations and pass information to the next layer. Deep learning models learn to adjust the weights and biases of these connections through a process known as backpropagation, where errors are propagated backward through the network to update the parameters and improve the model's performance.

The availability of large datasets, powerful hardware (such as graphics processing units or

GPUs), and advancements in algorithms have fueled the rapid progress of deep learning in recent years. Deep learning has revolutionized areas such as image and speech recognition, natural language understanding, and autonomous driving, leading to significant breakthroughs in AI applications.

3.1.6 Expert Systems

Expert Systems, also known as knowledge-based systems, are AI systems designed to mimic the problem-solving and decision-making abilities of human experts in specific domains. These systems are built on a knowledge base that contains expert knowledge and rules, which are used to reason and provide solutions to complex problems.

Expert systems rely on logical inference and pattern matching to analyze input data and apply the relevant knowledge to generate recommendations or make decisions. They are particularly useful in domains where human expertise is crucial, such as medical diagnosis, financial analysis, and troubleshooting complex systems.

While expert systems have been successful in certain domains, they are limited by their reliance on explicit knowledge representation and the challenges of capturing and maintaining expert knowledge. The development of expert systems often requires extensive collaboration between domain experts and AI researchers to ensure the accuracy and effectiveness of the system.

3.1.7 Natural Language Processing

Natural Language Processing (NLP) is a branch of AI that focuses on enabling computers to understand, interpret, and generate human language. NLP encompasses a wide range of tasks, including speech recognition, sentiment analysis, language translation, and text generation.

NLP systems utilize techniques from machine learning, deep learning, and linguistics to process and analyze natural language data. These systems aim to extract meaning from text or speech, understand context and intent, and generate human-like responses. NLP has found applications in various fields, such as virtual assistants, chatbots, language translation services, and information retrieval systems.

Advancements in deep learning, particularly the development of transformer models like GPT (Generative Pre-trained Transformer), have significantly improved the capabilities of NLP systems. These models can generate coherent and contextually relevant text, leading to more natural and engaging human-computer interactions.

3.1.8 Computer Vision

Computer Vision is a field of AI that focuses on enabling computers to interpret and understand visual information from images or videos. Computer vision algorithms aim to mimic human visual perception by extracting features, recognizing objects, and understanding the spatial relationships within visual data.

Computer vision has numerous applications, including image recognition, object detection and tracking, facial recognition, and scene understanding. It plays a vital role in various domains, such as autonomous vehicles, surveillance systems, medical imaging, and augmented reality.

Deep learning has revolutionized computer vision by enabling the development of deep neural networks, such as convolution neural networks (CNNs), which have achieved remarkable performance in image classification and object detection tasks. CNNs learn to extract hierarchical features from images, allowing them to recognize patterns and objects with high accuracy.

In recent years, computer vision has seen significant advancements in areas such as image segmentation, where algorithms can accurately identify and classify different regions within an image, and image generation, where generative models can create realistic and novel images based on training data. These advancements have paved the way for applications like autonomous driving, medical diagnostics, and visual content creation.

3.1.9 Robotics and Automation

AI has also played a crucial role in the advancement of robotics and automation. Robotic systems integrated with AI technologies can perceive their environment, make decisions, and perform physical tasks with precision and adaptability. These systems are used in various industries, including manufacturing, healthcare, agriculture, and logistics.

AI-powered robots often utilize computer vision, machine learning, and sensor technologies to navigate and interact with their surroundings. They can handle complex tasks such as object manipulation, grasping, and even decision-making in dynamic and unstructured environments. Robotic systems have the potential to increase efficiency, productivity, and safety in many industries, leading to the rise of smart factories, automated warehouses, and robotic-assisted surgeries.

3.1.10 Ethical and Responsible AI

As AI technologies continue to advance, ethical considerations and responsible practices become increasingly important. The rise of AI brings forth various challenges and concerns that need to be addressed to ensure the responsible and beneficial use of these technologies.

One significant ethical concern is the potential impact of AI on jobs and the workforce. Automation and AI-driven systems have the potential to replace certain job roles, leading to unemployment and economic disparities. It is crucial to focus on strategies for retraining and upskilling the workforce to adapt to the changing job landscape brought about by AI.

Another ethical consideration is the potential bias in AI systems. Machine learning models are trained on datasets that may contain inherent biases, leading to discriminatory outcomes. It is important to ensure that AI systems are trained on diverse and representative datasets and that algorithms are regularly audited to mitigate bias and ensure fairness and equity.

Privacy and data protection are also significant concerns in the age of AI. AI systems often rely on vast amounts of personal data to learn and make predictions. It is essential to establish robust data governance frameworks to protect individuals' privacy and ensure the responsible handling and storage of data.

Transparency and explainability are crucial for building trust in AI systems. As AI technologies become more complex and powerful, it becomes challenging to understand how decisions are made. Efforts are being made to develop methods and techniques that allow AI systems to provide explanations for their decisions and actions, enabling users to understand and verify the reasoning behind the system's outputs.

Finally, the safety and security of AI systems are paramount. As AI technologies become more autonomous and capable, ensuring their reliability and robustness becomes crucial. Steps need to be taken to prevent malicious use of AI and to develop mechanisms that guarantee the safety and security of AI systems in critical domains like healthcare, transportation, and defense.

To address these ethical concerns, policymakers, researchers, and industry leaders must collaborate to establish ethical frameworks, guidelines, and regulations that promote the responsible development, deployment, and use of AI technologies.

The rise of artificial intelligence has brought significant advancements and transformative changes to various fields. From narrow AI systems that excel in specific tasks to the pursuit of general and superintelligent AI, the capabilities of AI technologies continue to expand.

Machine learning, deep learning, expert systems, natural language processing, computer vision, and robotics are some of the key branches and applications of AI. These technologies have demonstrated remarkable achievements in areas such as image recognition, speech synthesis, autonomous driving, and medical diagnosis.

Advancements in AI Technologies: Unleashing the Power of Intelligent Automation

This article explores the recent advancements in artificial intelligence (AI) technologies and their impact on various industries. AI has undergone rapid evolution, enabling machines to simulate human intelligence, analyze complex data, and perform tasks with accuracy and efficiency. The article highlights key breakthroughs in AI, including machine learning, natural language processing, computer vision, and robotics. Furthermore, it discusses the applications of AI across diverse sectors such as healthcare, finance, manufacturing, and transportation. Finally, it examines the ethical considerations surrounding AI and the importance of responsible development and deployment. With AI technologies poised to transform our lives, understanding their advancements is crucial for harnessing their potential benefits while addressing potential challenges.

Artificial intelligence (AI) has emerged as a disruptive force that is reshaping the way we live and work. Over the past few decades, AI technologies have undergone significant advancements, driven by breakthroughs in computing power, data availability, and algorithmic innovations. This article aims to provide an overview of the recent advancements in AI technologies, highlighting their potential and applications across various industries.

Machine Learning: Empowering Intelligent Systems

Machine learning (ML) lies at the heart of AI advancements. ML algorithms enable machines to learn from data, identify patterns, and make predictions or decisions without being explicitly programmed. Recent advancements in ML have led to the development of deep learning models, capable of handling massive amounts of data and extracting complex features. Deep learning has revolutionized numerous domains, including image and speech recognition, natural language processing, and recommendation systems.

2.1 Deep Learning and Neural Networks

Deep learning models, based on artificial neural networks, have witnessed significant advancements. Convolutional Neural Networks (CNNs) have revolutionized computer vision tasks, enabling machines to accurately classify and recognize images. Recurrent Neural Networks (RNNs) and Transformer models have revolutionized natural language processing, allowing machines to understand and generate human-like text. The combination of deep learning and reinforcement learning has also led to breakthroughs in robotics and autonomous systems.

2.2 Transfer Learning and Federated Learning

Transfer learning has emerged as a powerful technique in AI, enabling the transfer of knowledge from one task or domain to another. Pretrained models such as BERT, GPT, and ImageNet have transformed various applications by providing a foundation for building customized AI solutions with limited labeled data. Federated learning has also gained attention, allowing models to be trained collaboratively across multiple devices or servers without sharing raw data, addressing privacy concerns.

Natural Language Processing: Bridging the Gap between Humans and Machines

Natural language processing (NLP) focuses on enabling machines to understand, interpret, and generate human language. Recent advancements in NLP have led to significant breakthroughs, making human-machine interactions more seamless and efficient.

3.1 Language Understanding and Generation

State-of-the-art language models, such as GPT (Generative Pre-trained Transformer) and BERT (Bidirectional Encoder Representations from Transformers), have transformed tasks such as text completion, translation, sentiment analysis, and question-answering. These models have brought about substantial improvements in machine translation, allowing for more accurate and context-aware translations.

3.2 Conversational AI and Chatbots

Conversational AI has witnessed notable advancements with the development of chatbots and virtual assistants. These systems leverage NLP techniques to engage in human-like conversations, providing customer support, information retrieval, and personalized recommendations. Chatbots have become an integral part of businesses, improving customer service and automating routine tasks.

Computer Vision: Enabling Machines to See and Understand

Computer vision involves the analysis and understanding of visual data, enabling machines to interpret images and videos. Recent advancements in computer vision have propelled AI technologies into applications such as autonomous vehicles, facial recognition, medical imaging, and augmented reality.

4.1 Object Detection and Recognition

Advancements in object detection algorithms, such as Faster R-CNN and YOLO (You Only Look Once), have greatly improved the accuracy and speed of detecting and localizing objects within images or videos. These techniques find applications in various fields, including autonomous driving, surveillance systems, and quality control in manufacturing.

4.2 Image and Video Understanding

With the development of deep learning models, machines can now understand and interpret the content of images and videos. Image classification, segmentation, and captioning techniques have improved significantly, enabling applications such as content moderation, visual search, and video analysis for security and entertainment purposes.

4.3 Medical Imaging and Diagnostics

Computer vision has made substantial contributions to the field of healthcare by enhancing medical imaging and diagnostics. Advanced algorithms can now analyze medical images such as X-rays, MRIs, and CT scans, assisting doctors in early detection and accurate diagnosis of diseases. Computer-aided diagnosis systems have improved the efficiency and reliability of medical imaging interpretation.

Robotics: Advancing Automation and Collaboration
Robotics, coupled with AI technologies, has witnessed remarkable advancements, revolutionizing industries that require automation, precision, and human-robot collaboration.

5.1 Industrial Automation and Manufacturing

AI-powered robots and cobots (collaborative robots) have transformed industrial automation and manufacturing processes. These robots can perform complex tasks with precision and efficiency, leading to increased productivity and reduced operational costs. They can adapt to changing environments, collaborate with humans, and handle repetitive or hazardous tasks.

5.2 Healthcare and Rehabilitation Robotics

Robotics has found extensive applications in healthcare, assisting in surgeries, rehabilitation, and patient care. Surgical robots offer increased precision and minimally invasive procedures, leading to faster recovery times and improved patient outcomes. Robotic exoskeletons aid in physical therapy and rehabilitation, enabling individuals with mobility impairments to regain independence.

5.3 Service Robots and Personal Assistants

AI-powered service robots and personal assistants are becoming increasingly common in various settings, including hotels, restaurants, and households. These robots can perform tasks such as cleaning, delivery, and customer service, enhancing convenience and efficiency in daily life.

AI in Industry Verticals

The advancements in AI technologies have permeated across various industry verticals, revolutionizing processes, and driving innovation. Let's explore some prominent examples:

6.1 Healthcare and Medicine

AI has made significant contributions to healthcare, ranging from diagnostics and drug discovery to patient monitoring and personalized medicine. Machine learning algorithms can analyze vast amounts of medical data, detect patterns, and aid in disease diagnosis and treatment planning. AI-based systems assist in predicting patient outcomes, optimizing resource allocation, and improving overall healthcare delivery.

6.2 Finance and Banking

AI has transformed the finance industry, automating processes, enhancing risk assessment, and improving customer experience. Machine learning algorithms analyze financial data for fraud detection, credit scoring, and investment strategies. Chatbots and virtual assistants provide personalized financial advice and support, making banking services more accessible and efficient.

6.3 Transportation and Logistics

The transportation and logistics sector has seen significant advancements with AI technologies. Autonomous vehicles, enabled by AI and computer vision, offer safer and more efficient transportation. AI algorithms optimize route planning, resource allocation, and supply chain management, reducing costs and improving delivery logistics.

6.4 Retail and E-commerce

AI is reshaping the retail industry by personalizing customer experiences, improving inventory management, and optimizing pricing strategies. Recommendation systems leverage AI algorithms to provide tailored product suggestions based on customer preferences and behavior. Computer vision enables cashier-less checkout systems and real-time inventory tracking, streamlining operations.

Ethical Considerations and Responsible AI Development

As AI technologies advance, it is essential to address the ethical considerations and ensure responsible development and deployment. The following aspects are crucial to consider:

7.1 Bias and Fairness

AI systems are trained on vast amounts of data, which can inadvertently contain biases. Biased data can lead to discriminatory outcomes, reinforcing existing inequalities. It is important to address bias and ensure fairness in AI algorithms, both in the data used for training and the decision-making processes of AI systems. Regular audits and evaluation of AI models can help identify and mitigate bias.

7.2 Privacy and Security

AI technologies often rely on extensive data collection and analysis, raising concerns about privacy and security. It is crucial to establish robust privacy frameworks and adhere to data protection regulations. Additionally, AI systems should be designed with built-in security measures to prevent unauthorized access or malicious use of sensitive information.

7.3 Transparency and Explainability

AI algorithms can be complex and difficult to interpret, leading to concerns about transparency and explainability. In certain domains, such as healthcare and finance, it is essential to understand how AI systems arrive at their decisions or recommendations. Research on explainable AI (XAI) aims to develop methods that provide transparency and insights into the decision-making processes of AI models.

7.4 Accountability and Liability

Determining accountability and liability in cases where AI systems cause harm or make erroneous decisions is a challenging issue. Clear guidelines and regulations are necessary to define the roles and responsibilities of developers, users, and the AI systems themselves. Ensuring mechanisms for redress and accountability can help mitigate potential risks associated with AI technologies.

7.5 Human-AI Collaboration

Rather than replacing human capabilities, AI technologies should be designed to augment human intelligence and support collaboration between humans and machines. This approach can lead to more effective and ethical applications of AI. Designing AI systems with user-centric principles and involving human feedback in the development process can enhance the usability and acceptance of AI technologies.

Future Directions and Challenges

While AI technologies have made remarkable advancements, several challenges and areas for future development remain:

8.1 General AI and AGI

The development of general artificial intelligence (AGI) that possesses human-level intelligence across various domains remains a long-term goal. AGI would have the ability to understand, learn, and adapt to new situations, leading to transformative applications. However, AGI development raises profound ethical and societal questions, requiring careful consideration and regulation.

8.2 Data Quality and Availability

The performance of AI systems heavily relies on the quality and availability of data. Ensuring high-quality, diverse, and representative datasets is crucial to avoid biases and improve the accuracy and generalizability of AI models. Additionally, efforts to address data scarcity in certain domains can further advance AI technologies.

8.3 Continual Learning and Adaptability

Enabling AI systems to learn continuously and adapt to new data and scenarios is an ongoing challenge. Current approaches often require retraining or fine-tuning models with updated data, which can be resource-intensive. Developing algorithms and architectures that can learn from limited or incremental data while retaining previous knowledge is an active area of research.

8.4 Interdisciplinary Collaboration and Regulation

AI development and deployment require collaboration among various disciplines, including computer science, ethics, law, and social sciences. Interdisciplinary collaboration can help address the complex challenges and potential risks associated with AI technologies. Additionally, international cooperation and regulations are necessary to ensure the responsible and ethical use of AI on a global scale.

Advancements in AI technologies have propelled us into an era of intelligent automation and transformation across industries. Machine learning, natural language processing, computer vision, and robotics have revolutionized the way we work, communicate, and interact with machines. As we harness the power of AI, it is vital to prioritize responsible development, addressing ethical considerations such as bias, privacy, and transparency. By embracing AI technologies and ensuring their responsible and ethical use, we can unlock their full potential to improve our lives and tackle complex challenges.

The recent advancements in AI have shown tremendous promise in various fields, from healthcare and finance to transportation and retail.

Machine learning algorithms have become more sophisticated, allowing machines to learn from data and make accurate predictions or decisions. Natural language processing has improved human-machine interactions, enabling machines to understand and generate human-like text. Computer vision has empowered machines to interpret visual data, opening up new possibilities in areas such as autonomous vehicles and medical imaging. Robotics has advanced automation and collaboration, leading to increased efficiency and improved safety.

However, as AI technologies continue to evolve, it is crucial to address ethical considerations and ensure responsible development and deployment. Bias in AI algorithms, data privacy and security, transparency and explainability, accountability and liability, and human-AI collaboration are key areas that require attention. Efforts should be made to minimize bias in AI systems, protect privacy and security, make AI algorithms transparent and explainable, establish accountability frameworks, and foster collaboration between humans and machines.

Moreover, future directions and challenges lie ahead in the AI landscape. The development of general artificial intelligence (AGI) remains a long-term goal, with profound ethical and societal implications. Ensuring data quality and availability, enabling continual learning and adaptability in AI systems, promoting interdisciplinary collaboration, and establishing international regulations are crucial for the responsible advancement of AI.

In conclusion, the advancements in AI technologies have paved the way for unprecedented opportunities and transformations in various industries. By harnessing the power of AI while addressing ethical considerations, we can leverage its potential to drive innovation, improve decision-making, enhance efficiency, and solve complex problems. The responsible development and deployment of AI technologies will shape the future and determine how we can reap the benefits while safeguarding the interests and well-being of individuals and society as a whole.

AI Applications in Various Fields

Artificial Intelligence (AI) has rapidly emerged as a transformative technology that is revolutionizing various fields and industries. With its ability to analyze vast amounts of data, learn from patterns, and make autonomous decisions, AI is driving innovation and efficiency across numerous domains. In this article, we will explore the applications of AI in various fields, highlighting its impact and potential for the future.

Healthcare:
AI is revolutionizing healthcare by enabling faster and more accurate diagnosis, personalized treatments, and improved patient care. Machine learning algorithms can analyze medical images, such as X-rays and MRIs, to detect abnormalities and assist radiologists in their diagnoses. Natural Language Processing (NLP) algorithms can mine through medical literature and patient records to

extract valuable insights, aiding in research and treatment plans. AI-powered chatbots and virtual assistants can also provide basic healthcare information, schedule appointments, and offer remote monitoring of patients, enhancing accessibility and reducing the burden on healthcare professionals.

Finance:
AI has transformed the financial industry by automating processes, improving risk assessment, and enhancing customer experiences. Machine learning algorithms can analyze vast amounts of financial data to detect patterns and predict market trends, helping traders and investors make informed decisions. AI-powered chatbots and virtual assistants can handle customer inquiries, provide personalized recommendations, and assist in managing financial portfolios. Fraud detection algorithms can identify suspicious transactions and prevent fraudulent activities, safeguarding the financial system.

Transportation:

AI is reshaping transportation systems by optimizing traffic flow, enhancing vehicle safety, and advancing autonomous vehicles. AI algorithms can analyze traffic data in real-time to optimize traffic signal timings, reduce congestion, and improve overall transportation efficiency. In the automotive industry, AI-powered systems enable advanced driver-assistance features, such as lane-keeping assistance and adaptive cruise control, enhancing vehicle safety. Furthermore, AI is a key enabler of autonomous vehicles, which have the potential to revolutionize transportation by reducing accidents, improving fuel efficiency, and providing increased accessibility for individuals with limited mobility.

Retail and E-commerce:

AI is transforming the retail and e-commerce sectors by providing personalized customer experiences, optimizing inventory management, and enhancing supply chain operations. Recommendation systems powered by AI algorithms can analyze customer data and browsing patterns to offer personalized product recommendations, increasing sales and customer satisfaction. AI-powered chatbots can provide real-time customer support, answering queries and assisting with purchase decisions. AI can also improve inventory management by predicting demand, optimizing stock levels, and reducing wastage. Additionally, AI-driven analytics can enhance supply chain operations by optimizing routes, predicting delivery times, and reducing costs.

Education:
AI is revolutionizing the education sector by personalizing learning experiences, automating administrative tasks, and enabling intelligent tutoring systems. Adaptive learning platforms powered by AI algorithms can tailor educational content to the needs and learning styles of

individual students, improving engagement and learning outcomes. AI-powered virtual tutors can provide personalized feedback, answer questions, and guide students through their studies. Administrative tasks, such as grading assignments and managing schedules, can be automated, freeing up time for teachers to focus on instruction and student support.

Manufacturing and Industry:
AI is driving innovation and efficiency in manufacturing and industry by optimizing processes, improving quality control, and enabling predictive maintenance. AI algorithms can analyze sensor data from manufacturing equipment to detect anomalies, predict failures, and schedule maintenance, reducing downtime and improving productivity. Machine learning algorithms can optimize production processes by analyzing data from various sources, identifying bottlenecks, and suggesting improvements. Computer vision systems

powered by AI can inspect products for defects, ensuring consistent quality control.

Agriculture:

AI is revolutionizing agriculture by enabling precision farming, optimizing crop yields, and improving resource management. AI algorithms can analyze data from sensors, satellites, and drones to provide farmers with insights into soil conditions, crop health, and weather patterns. This data-driven approach allows farmers to make informed decisions regarding irrigation, fertilization, and pest control, leading to optimized crop yields and reduced resource waste. AI-powered robots and drones can also assist in tasks such as planting, harvesting, and monitoring crops, increasing efficiency and reducing labor costs.

Energy and Utilities:

AI is playing a crucial role in the energy and utilities sector by optimizing energy generation, improving grid management, and promoting energy efficiency. AI algorithms can analyze energy consumption patterns and weather data to optimize energy generation and distribution, reducing costs and ensuring a stable power supply. Machine learning algorithms can also predict equipment failures and maintenance needs, enabling proactive maintenance and minimizing downtime. Furthermore, AI can help identify energy-saving opportunities by analyzing energy usage data and suggesting energy-efficient practices.

Cybersecurity:
AI is transforming cybersecurity by improving threat detection, enhancing response capabilities, and protecting against cyber threats. AI algorithms can analyze vast amounts of data and identify patterns that indicate potential cyber threats or anomalies. Machine learning models can continuously learn from new data to adapt and improve their detection capabilities. AI-powered systems can also automate incident response,

enabling faster and more efficient threat mitigation. Additionally, AI can assist in user authentication, network monitoring, and data encryption, bolstering overall cybersecurity measures.

Entertainment and Media:

AI is reshaping the entertainment and media industry by personalizing content recommendations, enhancing content creation, and enabling virtual reality experiences. AI-powered recommendation systems analyze user preferences and behaviors to offer personalized content suggestions, improving user engagement and satisfaction. Natural Language Processing algorithms can generate automated news articles or summaries, assist in content curation, and even create virtual news anchors. AI algorithms can also create realistic virtual reality experiences, enhancing gaming and entertainment options.

Environmental Sustainability:

AI is playing a vital role in promoting environmental sustainability by monitoring and managing natural resources, mitigating climate change impacts, and supporting conservation efforts. AI algorithms can analyze satellite imagery and sensor data to monitor deforestation, track wildlife populations, and detect illegal activities, aiding in conservation and environmental protection. Machine learning models can also predict climate change patterns, optimize energy consumption, and support sustainable urban planning.

Artificial Intelligence has become an integral part of various fields, revolutionizing industries, and transforming the way we live and work. Its applications in healthcare, finance, transportation, retail, education, manufacturing, agriculture, energy, cybersecurity, entertainment, and environmental sustainability are just a glimpse of its potential. As AI continues to evolve and advance, it is poised to create further breakthroughs and contribute to a more efficient, sustainable, and innovative future across multiple domains. However, it is essential to ensure ethical considerations, transparency, and responsible implementation of AI technologies to maximize their benefits while addressing potential challenges and risks.

Potential Negative Effects of AI on Human Intelligence

4.1 Overreliance on AI Systems

Artificial Intelligence (AI) systems have become an integral part of our daily lives, offering convenience, efficiency, and accuracy in various domains. From virtual personal assistants to recommendation algorithms, AI technologies have permeated almost every aspect of our society. While the positive impacts of AI are often highlighted, it is crucial to recognize and examine the potential negative effects that overreliance on AI systems can have on human intelligence. This section explores some of these effects, including the erosion of critical thinking skills, decreased creativity, and reduced human agency.

One of the primary concerns regarding overreliance on AI systems is the erosion of critical thinking skills. As individuals increasingly rely on AI to perform tasks and make decisions on their behalf, there is a risk of diminishing their ability to think critically and independently. AI systems are designed to analyze vast amounts of data and provide optimized solutions, often with high accuracy. However, this ease of access to ready-made answers can lead to a complacent mindset, where individuals no longer feel the need to question or evaluate the information presented to them.

Critical thinking is a fundamental aspect of human intelligence, enabling individuals to analyze, evaluate, and interpret information effectively. It involves skills such as logical reasoning, problem-solving, and the ability to assess the credibility and reliability of sources. Overreliance on AI systems can diminish these skills, as individuals become accustomed to accepting AI-generated results without engaging in the cognitive processes necessary for critical thinking.

Moreover, overreliance on AI systems can contribute to a decline in creativity. Creativity is a unique cognitive ability that sets humans apart from machines. It involves the generation of novel and valuable ideas, the ability to think outside the box, and the integration of disparate concepts. However, if individuals consistently depend on AI systems to provide solutions or creative insights, they may become less inclined to engage in creative thinking themselves.

AI algorithms are typically designed based on patterns and existing data, which limits their ability to generate truly innovative ideas. By relying solely on AI-generated suggestions or recommendations, individuals may miss out on the opportunity to explore uncharted territories, develop new ideas, or challenge established conventions. Creativity is a vital aspect of human intelligence that fuels innovation, artistic expression, and problem-solving in unique and imaginative ways. Therefore, a decline in creativity due to overreliance on AI systems could stifle human progress and limit our capacity for ingenuity.

Another negative effect of overreliance on AI systems is the potential reduction of human agency. Human agency refers to the ability to make independent choices, take action, and exert control over one's life and surroundings. As AI systems increasingly permeate various domains, such as autonomous vehicles, healthcare diagnosis, or financial decision-making, individuals may gradually surrender decision-making authority to AI algorithms.

While AI systems can provide efficient and accurate recommendations, they are ultimately based on predefined algorithms and programmed objectives. This can limit the range of options available to individuals and restrict their freedom to make choices based on personal values, intuition, or subjective factors. The more individuals rely on AI systems, the more they risk becoming passive recipients of AI-generated decisions, relinquishing their autonomy and agency.

Furthermore, overreliance on AI systems can lead to a phenomenon known as automation bias. Automation bias occurs when individuals unquestioningly trust the decisions or recommendations provided by automated systems, even when these decisions contradict their own judgment or intuition. This bias can be particularly problematic when AI systems are deployed in critical areas such as healthcare or public safety. If individuals blindly follow AI-generated suggestions without critical evaluation, it can have severe consequences, including medical misdiagnosis or incorrect legal decisions.

Additionally, overreliance on AI systems can exacerbate existing societal inequalities. AI algorithms are trained on historical data, which may contain biases and prejudices present in society. If individuals heavily rely on AI systems that perpetuate these biases, it can reinforce and amplify existing social inequalities. For example, if AI algorithms are used in the recruitment process, they may inadvertently favor certain demographic groups or penalize others based on historical patterns of discrimination. This can lead to a perpetuation of biased hiring practices and hinder efforts to achieve diversity and inclusion.

Moreover, overreliance on AI systems can result in a loss of specialized knowledge and skills. As AI technologies advance, there is a growing trend towards automation of tasks that were previously performed by humans. While this can lead to increased efficiency and productivity, it also means that individuals may no longer need to acquire or develop certain specialized skills. For example, with the rise of automated translation tools, the demand for human translators may decrease, reducing the incentive for individuals to invest time and effort in learning multiple languages.

This loss of specialized knowledge and skills can have broader implications for society. If certain professions or areas of expertise become obsolete due to automation, it can lead to unemployment and economic disparities. Furthermore, it may limit the diversity of perspectives and expertise available, as AI systems are designed based on the knowledge and biases of their creators. Human intelligence encompasses a wide range of skills and expertise, and overreliance on AI systems can narrow the scope of knowledge and limit the opportunities for individuals to develop and apply their unique abilities.

Additionally, overreliance on AI systems can have psychological and social implications. Human interaction and social connection are essential for emotional well-being and the development of social skills. However, the increasing integration of AI technologies in various aspects of life, such as chatbots or virtual companions, may lead to a substitution of human relationships with AI interactions. While AI systems can simulate human-like conversations and provide companionship to some extent, they lack the emotional depth, empathy, and genuine human connection that interpersonal relationships offer.

Relying too heavily on AI systems for emotional support or social interaction may lead to a sense of isolation, detachment, or even a devaluation of human relationships. This can have adverse effects on mental health and social cohesion, as individuals may become more reliant on AI companions rather than fostering meaningful connections with other humans. It is crucial to maintain a balance between the use of AI technologies and the preservation of human-to-human relationships to ensure overall well-being and social functioning.

In conclusion, while AI systems offer numerous benefits and advancements, it is essential to be aware of the potential negative effects that overreliance on these systems can have on human intelligence. Overreliance on AI can lead to the erosion of critical thinking skills, decreased creativity, reduced human agency, reinforcement of biases and inequalities, loss of specialized knowledge, and psychological and social implications. To mitigate these potential negative effects, it is important to approach AI as a tool and not a replacement for human intelligence. Striking a balance between leveraging AI technologies for their advantages and nurturing and developing our own cognitive abilities is crucial for maintaining and enhancing human intelligence in the age of AI.

4.2 Reduced Cognitive Abilities and Skills

While artificial intelligence (AI) has the potential to enhance human intelligence and augment our cognitive abilities, there is also a concern that it may lead to reduced cognitive abilities and skills among individuals. This section will explore some of the potential negative effects of AI on human intelligence in terms of reduced cognitive abilities and skills.

4.2.1 Overdependence on AI

One of the significant concerns related to the reduced cognitive abilities is the overdependence on AI systems. As AI technology becomes more advanced and integrated into various aspects of our lives, there is a risk that individuals may rely too heavily on AI systems for tasks that require critical thinking and problem-solving skills. This overreliance on AI could result in a decline in human cognitive abilities over time.

For example, consider the case of automated decision-making systems used in various fields such as healthcare, finance, and law. These systems can provide valuable insights and recommendations based on vast amounts of data and complex algorithms. However, if individuals solely rely on these systems without questioning their outputs or considering alternative perspectives, they may gradually lose their ability to critically analyze information and make independent decisions. This overdependence on AI systems may lead to a decline in human cognitive abilities related to reasoning, judgment, and decision-making.

4.2.2 Reduced Memory and Information Retention

Another potential negative effect of AI on human intelligence is the reduced reliance on our memory and information retention capabilities. With the advent of AI-powered personal assistants and search engines, individuals can easily access information on any topic with just a few clicks or voice commands. While this can be highly convenient and efficient, it may also lead to a decline in our ability to retain and recall information.

Research has shown that our memory and retention abilities are influenced by the frequency and intensity of information retrieval. When we repeatedly access information through external sources like search engines, our brains become less adept at storing and recalling that information. This phenomenon, known as the "Google effect" or "digital amnesia," suggests that reliance on AI for information retrieval may lead to a decline in our cognitive abilities related to memory and information retention.

Moreover, AI systems can personalize and filter information based on user preferences, potentially creating information bubbles that reinforce existing beliefs and limit exposure to diverse perspectives. This could further contribute to a reduction in critical thinking and open-mindedness, as individuals may become less inclined to actively seek out new information and challenge their existing knowledge.

4.2.3 Diminished Problem-Solving Skills

AI systems are designed to solve complex problems efficiently by analyzing large datasets and applying sophisticated algorithms. While this can undoubtedly be beneficial in many domains, there is a concern that individuals may become less adept at solving problems independently as they rely more on AI systems.

When AI systems provide quick and accurate solutions to problems, individuals may be less motivated to engage in problem-solving activities themselves. This reduced engagement in problem-solving could lead to a decline in cognitive abilities related to creativity, critical thinking, and innovative problem-solving approaches.

Moreover, AI systems often operate as black boxes, meaning that their decision-making processes are not easily understandable or explainable to humans. This lack of transparency can make it difficult for individuals to learn from AI systems and improve their problem-solving skills. If individuals do not have a clear understanding of how AI arrives at its solutions, they may struggle to develop their own problem-solving strategies and techniques.

4.2.4 Deterioration of Social and Emotional Intelligence

Human intelligence is not solely based on cognitive abilities but also encompasses social and emotional intelligence. Social intelligence refers to the capacity to understand and navigate social interactions effectively, while emotional intelligence involves the ability to recognize, understand, and manage one's own emotions and the emotions of others.

While AI systems can analyze vast amounts of data and mimic certain aspects of human behavior, they lack the nuanced understanding and empathy that is inherent in human social and emotional intelligence. Therefore, overreliance on AI systems may contribute to the deterioration of these essential human abilities.

When individuals interact primarily with AI-powered virtual assistants or engage in online communication platforms, they may have fewer opportunities to practice and develop their social and emotional intelligence. These interactions often lack the non-verbal cues, emotional nuances, and empathetic responses that are present in face-to-face human interactions. As a result, individuals may become less skilled in interpreting and responding to social and emotional cues, which are crucial for building meaningful relationships and effective communication.

Additionally, AI systems are not equipped to understand and address the complexities of human emotions. They may lack the ability to provide genuine empathy and emotional support, which can be vital in various contexts such as counseling, therapy, and interpersonal relationships. Over time, excessive reliance on AI systems for emotional support and social interactions may lead to a decline in individuals' social and emotional intelligence, potentially resulting in difficulties in forming and maintaining interpersonal connections.

4.2.5 Loss of Manual and Practical Skills

AI technology has also made significant advancements in automating manual and practical tasks that were traditionally performed by humans.

While this automation brings efficiency and convenience, it also poses a risk of reducing human engagement in these activities, leading to a loss of manual and practical skills.

For instance, the increasing use of AI-powered autonomous vehicles may eventually lead to a decline in individuals' driving skills. As more people rely on self-driving cars, their ability to handle various driving scenarios and respond to unexpected situations may deteriorate. This loss of manual driving skills could potentially impact individuals' overall motor skills and situational awareness.

Similarly, the automation of manufacturing and assembly processes using AI-powered robots may reduce the need for human involvement in such tasks. As a result, individuals may have fewer opportunities to develop and hone their practical skills related to manual dexterity, hand-eye coordination, and problem-solving in a physical environment.

The loss of manual and practical skills not only affects individuals' ability to perform specific tasks but also has broader implications for creativity, adaptability, and the ability to work in dynamic environments. Practical skills are often intertwined with cognitive abilities, and the diminishing importance of these skills due to AI automation may lead to a decline in individuals' overall cognitive abilities.

4.2.6 Education and Skill Gaps

The potential negative effects of AI on human intelligence also extend to the education system and the development of essential skills. With the rise of AI in various industries, there is a growing concern that the skills required in the job market may shift, leaving individuals with outdated skills and knowledge.

AI systems are increasingly being used in educational settings to support learning and instruction. While this can enhance educational experiences in many ways, it may also lead to a reduced emphasis on certain cognitive abilities and skills. For example, if AI systems primarily focus on providing correct answers rather than fostering critical thinking, creativity, and problem-solving skills, students may not develop these essential abilities to the same extent.

Moreover, the rapid pace at which AI technology evolves poses a challenge for educational institutions to keep up with the changing demands of the job market. If the education system fails to adapt and provide relevant training and skills development opportunities, there is a risk of creating a significant skill gap between what AI systems can accomplish and what humans are capable of doing. This skill gap could result in reduced employment prospects and hinder individuals' ability to thrive in an AI-driven society.

Furthermore, there is a concern that AI technology may exacerbate existing inequalities in access to education and skills development. Affluent individuals and communities with better access to AI resources and technology may have a competitive advantage in acquiring the skills necessary to succeed in an AI-dominated world. This could widen the gap between the privileged and the disadvantaged, further marginalizing individuals who lack access to AI resources and training opportunities.

4.2.7 Ethical and Social Implications

The potential negative effects of AI on human intelligence also raise important ethical and social implications. As AI systems become more sophisticated and integrated into various aspects of our lives, there are concerns about the potential for bias, discrimination, and privacy infringements.

AI systems are trained on vast datasets that often reflect the biases and prejudices present in society. If these biases are not adequately addressed, AI systems can perpetuate and amplify existing societal inequalities. For example, if AI algorithms are used in hiring processes, they may inadvertently discriminate against certain demographic groups based on historical biases in the training data. This can lead to reduced opportunities for individuals from marginalized communities and hinder social progress.

Additionally, the widespread use of AI systems raises privacy concerns. AI technology relies on collecting and analyzing large amounts of personal data to make informed decisions and recommendations. The extensive data collection and surveillance required by AI systems may compromise individuals' privacy and autonomy.

This can have implications for cognitive autonomy, as individuals may feel pressured to conform to the recommendations and decisions made by AI systems, limiting their independent thought and decision-making abilities.

Furthermore, there is a growing concern about the impact of AI on employment and the labor market. As AI systems automate various tasks and job roles, there is a risk of significant job displacement, particularly in industries that heavily rely on routine and repetitive tasks. The loss of jobs and the need for retraining and reskilling to adapt to the changing job market can have profound effects on individuals' cognitive abilities, job security, and overall well-being.

4.2.8 Psychological Impact

The potential negative effects of AI on human intelligence also extend to the psychological well-being of individuals. Excessive reliance on AI systems for various tasks and decision-making can lead to a sense of learned helplessness and reduced self-efficacy.

Learned helplessness refers to a state in which individuals perceive themselves as powerless and incapable of influencing or controlling their environment. When individuals consistently rely on AI systems to solve problems or make decisions, they may begin to doubt their own abilities and lose confidence in their cognitive skills. This can have detrimental effects on motivation, creativity, and overall mental well-being.

Moreover, the increasing integration of AI systems in social interactions and online platforms may contribute to feelings of isolation and disconnection. While AI-powered virtual assistants and chatbots can simulate human-like interactions, they lack the depth and authenticity of genuine human connections. Prolonged exposure to AI-driven interactions may lead to a sense of social isolation, impacting individuals' emotional intelligence and overall psychological health.

In conclusion, while artificial intelligence has the potential to enhance human intelligence and augment our cognitive abilities, there are concerns about the potential negative effects on human cognitive abilities and skills. Overdependence on AI, reduced memory and information retention, diminished problem-solving skills, deterioration of social and emotional intelligence, loss of manual and practical skills, education and skill gaps, ethical and social implications, and psychological impact are among the potential negative consequences of AI on human intelligence. It is crucial to carefully consider and address these concerns to ensure that AI technology is developed and deployed in a manner that maximizes its benefits while minimizing its potential drawbacks.

4.3 Loss of Critical Thinking and Problem-Solving Skills

One potential negative effect of artificial intelligence (AI) on human intelligence is the loss of critical thinking and problem-solving skills. As AI becomes more prevalent in various aspects of our lives, there is a concern that humans may rely too heavily on AI systems to solve problems and make decisions, thereby diminishing their own cognitive abilities in these areas.

Critical thinking is the ability to objectively analyze and evaluate information to form a reasoned judgment or decision. It involves skills such as logical reasoning, evidence-based thinking, and the ability to consider multiple perspectives. Similarly, problem-solving skills refer to the capacity to identify and define problems, generate and evaluate potential solutions, and implement the most appropriate course of action.

Overdependence on AI Systems:

With the increasing capabilities of AI systems, there is a risk that individuals may become overly reliant on them for critical thinking and problem-solving tasks. For example, AI-powered recommendation systems are widely used in various domains, such as shopping, entertainment, and news consumption. These systems use algorithms to analyze user preferences and make personalized recommendations. While they can enhance convenience and efficiency, users may gradually lose their ability to critically evaluate information and make independent decisions. They may become passive recipients of recommendations without actively engaging in the decision-making process.

Reduction in Cognitive Effort:

AI systems often provide quick and efficient solutions to complex problems. This convenience may lead individuals to avoid engaging in the cognitive effort required for critical thinking and problem-solving. When confronted with a challenging task, individuals may be tempted to rely on AI systems rather than investing the time and effort to analyze the problem themselves. This can result in a gradual erosion of their cognitive skills in these areas.

Narrowing of Perspective:

AI algorithms are designed to analyze large amounts of data and make predictions or decisions based on patterns and correlations. While this can be beneficial in many contexts, it also has the potential to narrow human perspectives. If individuals solely rely on AI-generated recommendations or decisions, they may become confined to a limited set of options or perspectives. This can hinder their ability to think critically, consider alternative viewpoints, and come up with creative solutions to complex problems.

Loss of Analytical Skills:

AI systems excel in processing and analyzing vast amounts of data at a speed far beyond human capabilities. As a result, humans may gradually lose their analytical skills as they rely on AI systems to perform data analysis tasks. This can be particularly concerning in fields such as research, where critical thinking and analytical skills are essential for making groundbreaking discoveries. If researchers rely heavily on AI algorithms to analyze data, they may become detached from the underlying principles and processes, leading to a decline in their ability to interpret and draw meaningful insights from the data.

Reduced Cognitive Flexibility:
Critical thinking and problem-solving skills require cognitive flexibility, which is the ability to adapt one's thinking and approach based on changing circumstances. AI systems often operate within predefined parameters and algorithms, which may limit their ability to adapt to new or unexpected situations. If individuals rely heavily on AI systems

for decision-making and problem-solving, they may become less adept at adapting their thinking to novel or complex scenarios. This can hinder their ability to think critically, consider alternative approaches, and come up with creative solutions.

Weakening of Memory and Attention:
AI technologies, such as virtual assistants and smart devices, provide easy access to information and perform tasks that previously required human effort. While this can enhance productivity and convenience, it may also lead to a decline in human memory and attention capacities. If individuals constantly rely on AI systems to store and retrieve information, they may become less skilled at retaining and recalling information from their own memory. Moreover, the constant availability of AI-based solutions may reduce the need for sustained attention and concentration, potentially leading to a decrease in individuals' ability to focus and engage in deep thinking.

Decreased Cognitive Effort Allocation:

When AI systems take over certain cognitive tasks, individuals may allocate less cognitive effort to those tasks, resulting in a decline in their overall cognitive abilities. For example, automated spelling and grammar checkers in word processors have made it easier for individuals to produce error-free written content. While this can save time and improve the quality of written work, it may also reduce individuals' motivation to develop and practice their own language skills. The reliance on AI systems for these tasks may lead to a deterioration in spelling and grammar abilities over time.

Lack of Understanding of AI Processes:

As AI systems become more sophisticated, their inner workings become increasingly complex and opaque to the average user. This lack of understanding can contribute to a loss of critical thinking and problem-solving skills. When individuals rely on AI systems to make decisions or provide recommendations, they may not fully comprehend the underlying algorithms, data sources, or biases that influence the system's output. This lack of transparency can prevent individuals from critically evaluating the reliability and validity of the AI-generated information, potentially leading to uninformed decisions or misguided actions.

Decreased Motivation for Learning:
The availability of AI systems that can quickly provide answers or solutions may diminish individuals' motivation to engage in deep learning and exploration. When faced with a question or problem, individuals may opt for the immediate gratification of an AI-generated answer rather than investing the time and effort to research and understand the topic themselves. This can result in a decline in individuals' motivation for learning, as they rely on AI systems to provide instant information without actively engaging in the process of acquiring knowledge.

Loss of Social Skills:

As AI technologies become more integrated into daily life, there is a concern that individuals may rely less on human interactions for problem-solving and decision-making. This can have detrimental effects on the development of social skills, such as effective communication, collaboration, and negotiation. When individuals predominantly interact with AI systems for critical thinking tasks, they may lose the opportunity to engage in meaningful discussions, debates, and exchanges of ideas with other humans. This can lead to a decline in their ability to understand different perspectives, empathize with others, and work effectively in collaborative environments.

Mitigating the Negative Effects:

While there are potential negative effects of AI on human intelligence, it is important to note that these effects are not inevitable. There are steps that can be taken to mitigate these negative impacts and ensure a healthy integration of AI with human cognitive abilities:

Promoting AI Literacy: It is crucial to enhance public understanding of AI systems, their limitations, and their potential biases. By promoting AI literacy, individuals can develop a more informed and critical perspective when using AI technologies. This can empower them to actively engage with AI systems while maintaining their own critical thinking and problem-solving skills.

Balancing AI and Human Effort: Encouraging individuals to strike a balance between relying on AI systems and engaging in independent critical thinking and problem-solving can help maintain and enhance their cognitive abilities. By consciously allocating effort to tasks that require active cognitive engagement, individuals can continue to develop and exercise their critical thinking skills.

Education Emphasizing Cognitive Skills: Educational institutions play a vital role in equipping individuals with the necessary cognitive skills to navigate the AI-driven world. Emphasizing critical thinking, problem-solving, and analytical skills in curricula can help counteract the potential loss of these abilities due to overdependence on AI systems.

Fostering Creativity and Innovation: While AI systems can provide efficient solutions, humans still possess unique capabilities in creativity and innovation. Encouraging individuals to think outside the box, explore diverse perspectives, and engage in creative problem-solving can help preserve and strengthen these cognitive abilities.

Ethical AI Development:
Promoting ethical practices in AI development is essential to mitigate the potential negative effects on human intelligence. Developers and researchers should prioritize transparency, fairness, and

accountability in the design and implementation of AI systems. By ensuring that AI algorithms are unbiased, explainable, and accountable, individuals can have more confidence in the decisions and recommendations provided by these systems. This can encourage users to engage in critical thinking and consider the limitations and potential biases of AI systems.

Continuous Learning and Adaptation: Individuals should cultivate a mindset of lifelong learning and adaptability to keep up with the advancements in AI technology. By staying informed about the latest developments, individuals can understand the capabilities and limitations of AI systems and make informed decisions about when and how to use them. This continuous learning can help individuals stay intellectually engaged and maintain their critical thinking and problem-solving skills.

Emphasizing Human Interaction: Despite the convenience and efficiency of AI systems, it is important to prioritize human interaction and collaboration in problem-solving and decision-making processes. Actively seeking diverse perspectives, engaging in meaningful discussions, and working in teams can foster critical thinking, empathy, and social skills that AI systems cannot replicate. By maintaining a balance between AI-driven solutions and human interaction, individuals can develop a more holistic approach to problem-solving.

Augmentation rather than Replacement: Instead of viewing AI as a complete replacement for human intelligence, it can be seen as a tool for augmentation. AI systems can assist and support human cognitive abilities, providing valuable insights and assistance in complex tasks. By leveraging AI as a complementary tool, individuals can enhance their problem-solving and decision-making capabilities while retaining their own critical thinking skills.

Ethical Use of AI: It is crucial to promote and enforce ethical guidelines and regulations for the use of AI systems. This includes ensuring privacy protection, preventing misuse of AI technology, and addressing potential biases and discrimination in AI algorithms. By fostering a responsible and ethical AI ecosystem, the negative effects on human intelligence can be minimized, and the benefits of AI can be maximized.

While artificial intelligence offers numerous benefits and advancements in various domains, it is important to be aware of the potential negative effects on human intelligence. The loss of critical thinking and problem-solving skills is a significant concern as individuals may become overly reliant on AI systems, leading to a decline in their cognitive abilities. However, by promoting AI literacy, maintaining a balance between AI and human effort, emphasizing cognitive skills in education, fostering creativity and innovation, ensuring ethical AI development, engaging in continuous learning, prioritizing human interaction, and promoting the ethical use of AI, these negative effects can be mitigated. It is crucial to approach the integration of AI with human intelligence in a thoughtful and responsible manner to ensure a harmonious coexistence that maximizes the benefits and minimizes the potential drawbacks.

4.4 Implications for Education and Learning

Education and learning are fundamental aspects of human development and progress. They shape our understanding of the world, equip us with skills, and foster critical thinking. However, the rise of artificial intelligence (AI) poses potential negative effects on human intelligence in the realm of education and learning. While AI has the potential to enhance certain aspects of education, such as personalized learning and efficient data analysis, it also raises concerns about the impact on human creativity, critical thinking, and social interaction. In this section, we will explore the implications of AI in education and learning and discuss its potential negative effects on human intelligences.

4.4.1 Overreliance on AI-based Learning Systems

One of the potential negative effects of AI in education is the overreliance on AI-based learning systems. As AI technologies become more advanced and accessible, there is a risk of educational institutions relying too heavily on automated systems for teaching and assessment. While these systems can provide personalized learning experiences and instant feedback, they may undermine the importance of human interaction and guidance in the learning process.

Human teachers play a crucial role in fostering critical thinking, creativity, and social skills. They can adapt their teaching methods to individual students, provide mentorship, and engage students in meaningful discussions. AI-based learning systems, on the other hand, are limited in their ability to understand the nuanced needs of students and provide personalized support beyond pre-defined algorithms. This overreliance on AI may lead to a reduction in the quality of education and hinder the development of essential human intelligences.

4.4.2 Narrowing of Curricula and Skillsets

AI has the potential to automate certain tasks and processes, leading to concerns about the narrowing of curricula and skillsets in education. As AI takes over routine tasks, there might be a tendency to prioritize the teaching of skills that are directly relevant to AI development and implementation. This could result in a neglect of other important areas of knowledge and skills that are vital for human intelligences, such as creativity, emotional intelligence, and critical thinking.

AI systems are designed to optimize efficiency and productivity, which may lead to a focus on measurable outcomes and standardized assessments. This approach may undervalue subjective aspects of learning and neglect the development of skills that are difficult to quantify. As a result, there is a risk of education becoming overly focused on narrow skillsets that align with AI automation, potentially neglecting the cultivation of broader human intelligences.

4.4.3 Threat to Creativity and Originality

Creativity is a distinctly human capability that has played a pivotal role in shaping our societies and advancing knowledge. However, the integration of AI in education raises concerns about its impact on human creativity and originality. AI systems are proficient in analyzing vast amounts of data and identifying patterns, but they struggle with generating truly novel and creative ideas.

In the context of education, AI-based systems may prioritize standardized answers and predefined solutions, potentially stifling students' creativity and discouraging them from exploring unconventional ideas. The emphasis on standardized assessments and predetermined benchmarks may discourage students from taking risks, experimenting, and thinking outside the box.

This could result in a generation of students who are less inclined to pursue creative endeavors and are limited in their ability to solve complex problems in innovative ways.

4.4.4 Social Isolation and Reduced Collaboration

Another potential negative effect of AI in education is the risk of increased social isolation and reduced collaboration among students. The integration of AI systems in classrooms may lead to a shift towards individualized learning experiences, where students primarily interact with machines rather than with their peers. While personalized learning can have benefits, it is crucial to recognize the importance of social interaction and collaboration in the educational process.

Human intelligence is not solely about individual knowledge and skills; it also encompasses the ability to communicate, collaborate, and work effectively in teams. In traditional educational settings, students engage in group activities, discussions, and projects that foster social skills, teamwork, and the exchange of diverse perspectives. However, the increasing reliance on AI-based learning systems may diminish these opportunities for social interaction.

AI systems lack the capacity for human empathy, emotional connection, and social nuances. The absence of human interaction in education may lead to a lack of social skills development and an increased sense of isolation among students. Collaborative problem-solving, negotiation, and effective communication are essential skills that are best cultivated through interpersonal interactions. Depriving students of these opportunities may hinder their overall development and limit their ability to navigate social dynamics in various contexts.

4.4.5 Ethical Concerns and Bias

AI technologies are not neutral entities but reflect the biases and values embedded in their design and training data. When integrated into educational systems, AI may perpetuate biases and reinforce existing social inequalities. For example, if AI algorithms are trained on biased data, they may inadvertently discriminate against certain groups of students based on race, gender, or socioeconomic status.

Furthermore, the use of AI in education raises ethical concerns regarding student privacy and data security. AI systems collect vast amounts of data on students' learning patterns, preferences, and behaviors. This data can be vulnerable to misuse, unauthorized access, or commercial exploitation. Inadequate protection of student data raises concerns about privacy violations and potential harm to individuals.

These ethical concerns can have negative implications for human intelligences in education.

Students need a safe and inclusive learning environment where their individuality is respected, their privacy is protected, and their unique strengths are nurtured.

.4.8 Lack of Human Judgment and Intuition

Human judgment and intuition are valuable cognitive abilities that are difficult to replicate in AI systems. In education, human teachers often rely on their experience, intuition, and contextual understanding to make informed decisions, provide guidance, and adapt their teaching methods to the specific needs of students. AI-based learning systems, although efficient in data analysis and pattern recognition, lack the depth of human judgment and the ability to navigate complex and nuanced situations.

Educational decisions such as identifying struggling students, offering personalized support, and providing emotional guidance require a level of empathy and understanding that AI systems currently cannot match. Relying solely on AI for decision-making in education may lead to a reduction in the quality and effectiveness of educational interventions, potentially overlooking the individual needs and circumstances of students.

4.4.9 Inequality and Accessibility Issues

While AI has the potential to enhance educational opportunities, it also poses challenges in terms of inequality and accessibility. The integration of AI technologies in education requires significant infrastructure, resources, and technical expertise. This may create disparities between well-funded schools or institutions that can afford advanced AI systems and those with limited resources or in disadvantaged areas.

Moreover, AI-based learning systems rely heavily on digital platforms and internet connectivity. This can create accessibility issues for students who do not have reliable internet access or lack access to necessary devices. As a result, students from marginalized communities or low-income backgrounds may face additional barriers to accessing quality education that incorporates AI technologies, further exacerbating educational inequalities.

Addressing the potential negative effects of AI in education and learning requires careful consideration and proactive measures. It is important to strike a balance between the integration of AI technologies and the preservation of essential aspects of human intelligence. Here are some strategies that can help mitigate the potential negative effects:

Emphasize the role of human teachers: Human teachers play a crucial role in education and should not be replaced by AI systems. Efforts should be made to support teachers in integrating AI technologies as tools to enhance their teaching methods, rather than relying solely on automated systems.

Foster a well-rounded education: Curricula should prioritize the development of essential human intelligences, such as creativity, critical thinking, and social skills. While AI can assist in certain areas, it is important to maintain a balanced approach that values a broad range of knowledge and skills.

Ensure ethical use of AI: Clear guidelines and ethical frameworks should be established to address issues of bias, privacy, and data security in the use of AI technologies in education. Transparency and accountability are key to mitigating potential harm and ensuring fair and equitable educational practices.

Promote collaboration and social interaction: Efforts should be made to maintain and enhance opportunities for social interaction, collaboration, and teamwork in educational settings. AI technologies can be utilized to facilitate group projects, discussions, and peer-to-peer learning experiences.

Develop digital literacy and critical thinking skills: Students should be equipped with the necessary skills to navigate AI technologies effectively. This includes developing digital literacy, critical thinking, and information evaluation skills to ensure they can critically analyze and interpret AI-generated content.

Encourage a growth mindset: Students should be encouraged to embrace challenges, take risks, and develop a growth mindset. This can help them adapt to the changing landscape of AI technologies and continue to cultivate their human intelligences.

Bridge the digital divide: Efforts should be made to bridge the digital divide and ensure equal access to AI-based educational resources. This includes providing reliable internet access, necessary devices, and technical support to students from disadvantaged backgrounds.

Bias and Limitations in AI Systems

5.1 Bias in AI Algorithms

Artificial Intelligence (AI) systems have the potential to transform various aspects of our lives, from healthcare and finance to transportation and entertainment. However, these systems are not immune to biases, which can lead to unfair outcomes and perpetuate societal inequalities. Bias in AI algorithms is a critical issue that needs to be addressed to ensure the ethical and responsible development and deployment of AI technologies.

Bias in AI algorithms refers to the systematic and unfair favoritism or discrimination that can occur when AI systems are trained on biased data or designed with inherent biases. These biases can emerge at different stages of the AI development process, including data collection, preprocessing, algorithm design, and decision-making. It is crucial to understand and mitigate bias in AI algorithms to ensure that these systems do not amplify existing social, cultural, or economic disparities.

There are several types of biases that can manifest in AI algorithms. Let's explore some of the most common ones:

Data Bias: AI algorithms are trained on large datasets, and if these datasets contain biased information, the resulting algorithms can inherit and perpetuate those biases. Data bias can occur due to various reasons, such as underrepresentation or overrepresentation of certain groups in the training data, sampling biases, or historical societal biases reflected in the data. For example, if a facial recognition algorithm is trained predominantly on data from light-skinned individuals, it may perform poorly when identifying faces of individuals with darker skin tones.

Algorithmic Bias: Bias can also arise from the algorithms themselves. Algorithmic bias occurs when the design, assumptions, or mathematical operations of an AI algorithm lead to biased outcomes. This bias can be unintentional, resulting from the complexity of the algorithm or the limitations of the data used for training. For instance, a predictive policing algorithm trained on historical crime data may inadvertently reinforce existing biases by targeting certain neighborhoods or demographic groups.

Interaction Bias: Interaction bias occurs when the AI system's behavior or responses vary depending on the characteristics of the user. It can be unintentional or intentional, arising from the biases present in the training data or explicitly programmed into the system. For example, a chatbot designed to assist customers may exhibit gender bias by responding differently or providing biased information based on the gender of the user.

Feedback Loop Bias: Feedback loop bias, also known as self-reinforcing bias, occurs when the outputs of an AI system are used as feedback to further train or fine-tune the system, leading to a perpetuation of biases. If the initial training data contains biased patterns, the algorithm may amplify and reinforce those biases through iterative feedback loops. This can result in a system that becomes increasingly biased over time.

The consequences of bias in AI algorithms can be far-reaching and have serious implications for individuals and society as a whole. Here are some key concerns associated with bias in AI:

Unfair Treatment: Bias in AI algorithms can lead to discriminatory outcomes, where certain individuals or groups are systematically disadvantaged or excluded. For example, biased credit scoring algorithms can result in unfair loan denials or higher interest rates for marginalized communities, perpetuating socioeconomic disparities.

Reinforcement of Stereotypes: Biased AI algorithms can reinforce and perpetuate harmful stereotypes. If AI systems are trained on biased data that reflects societal prejudices, they may learn and reproduce those biases in their decision-making processes. This can further marginalize already disadvantaged groups and hinder efforts towards achieving equality and inclusivity.

Lack of Diversity and Representation: Biased AI algorithms can contribute to the underrepresentation or erasure of certain groups. If a recommendation system suggests content based on biased user preferences, it can limit exposure to diverse perspectives, reinforcing echo chambers and further polarizing societal discourse.

Ineffective Solutions: Bias in AI algorithms can undermine the effectiveness of AI systems.

5.2 Limitations in AI Decision-Making

While AI systems have shown remarkable capabilities in various domains, they also suffer from certain limitations and biases in decision-making. These limitations can arise due to a variety of factors, including the quality and quantity of training data, the design of the AI algorithms, and the inherent biases present in society. In this section, we will explore some of the key limitations in AI decision-making and their potential consequences.

5.2.1 Lack of Common Sense Reasoning

One significant limitation in AI decision-making is the lack of common sense reasoning. AI models often struggle to make decisions that may seem obvious to humans but require a deeper understanding of context and common sense. For example, a language model trained solely on textual data may not be able to comprehend the nuances and cultural references required to interpret and respond appropriately to certain questions or statements. This limitation can lead to inaccurate or nonsensical responses, which can be problematic in applications such as customer support or legal document analysis.

The lack of common sense reasoning also becomes apparent in image recognition tasks. While AI models have made significant progress in object recognition, they still struggle with understanding complex scenes or inferring implicit information from images. For instance, an AI system might correctly identify a cat in a picture but fail to recognize that the cat is sitting on a chair. These limitations highlight the need for further research and development in incorporating common sense reasoning into AI systems.

5.2.2 Data Bias and Representational Bias
AI systems learn from the data they are trained on, and if the training data is biased, the resulting AI

model can also exhibit biased behavior. Bias in AI systems can stem from various sources, including biased training data, biased labels, or biased decisions made by human annotators during the training process. This can have serious consequences, as biased AI systems can perpetuate and amplify existing societal biases, leading to unfair or discriminatory outcomes.

Data bias can occur when the training data is not representative of the real-world population or contains systematic biases. For example, if an AI system is trained to predict loan eligibility based on historical loan data, and the training data disproportionately represents certain demographics or discriminates against protected classes, the AI system may learn to make biased decisions. This can result in unfair lending practices that disproportionately affect marginalized groups.

Representational bias refers to biases that arise from the design or structure of the AI system itself.

It can occur when the features or attributes used by the AI model to make decisions reflect or amplify societal biases. For instance, if a facial recognition system is primarily trained on data from light-skinned individuals, it may have difficulty accurately recognizing and categorizing individuals with darker skin tones. This can lead to biased outcomes, such as misidentifications or higher error rates for certain racial or ethnic groups.

Addressing data bias and representational bias requires careful attention to the data used for training, rigorous evaluation of AI models for bias, and the development of mitigation strategies. It is essential to have diverse and representative training datasets, unbiased labeling processes, and regular monitoring of AI systems in real-world applications to identify and rectify biases.

5.2.3 Lack of Explainability

Another significant limitation in AI decision-making is the lack of explainability. Many

AI models, particularly deep learning models, are often considered black boxes, meaning that their decision-making process is not readily understandable by humans. This lack of explainability can be problematic, especially in critical domains such as healthcare, finance, and legal systems, where the ability to explain and justify decisions is essential.

Explainability is crucial for establishing trust in AI systems and ensuring accountability. When an AI system makes a decision, it is crucial to understand how and why that decision was reached. However, deep learning models, with their complex architectures and numerous parameters, can be difficult to interpret and explain. The decision-making process of these models often involves intricate computations across multiple layers, making it challenging to trace the reasoning behind a specific decision.

The lack of explainability in AI decision-making can lead to several issues. First, it hinders the ability to identify and rectify errors or biases in the model's decision-making process. If an AI system makes a discriminatory decision or provides an incorrect diagnosis in healthcare, it is crucial to understand why that decision was made in order to correct it and prevent future occurrences.

Second, the lack of explainability can also impede user trust and acceptance of AI systems. Users, especially in sensitive domains, may be reluctant to rely on AI recommendations or decisions if they cannot understand or validate the underlying reasoning. This can limit the adoption and effectiveness of AI systems in various applications.

Researchers and practitioners are actively working on developing methods and techniques to enhance the explainability of AI systems. Explainable AI (XAI) is an emerging field that focuses on creating interpretable and transparent models that can provide explanations for their decisions. Techniques such as rule-based models, symbolic reasoning, and attention mechanisms are being explored to enable better understanding and interpretation of AI decisions.

In addition to developing explainable AI models, it is crucial to establish standards and regulations that require transparency and accountability in AI decision-making. Regulatory frameworks can ensure that AI systems are designed and deployed in a manner that allows for explainability and audibility. This includes requirements for documenting the decision-making process, providing transparency about the data used for training, and allowing individuals to challenge and understand the decisions made by AI systems.

5.2.4 Adversarial Attacks

Adversarial attacks are a significant limitation in AI decision-making, particularly in the field of computer vision. Adversarial attacks involve intentionally manipulating input data to deceive or mislead AI models. By making subtle changes to input images or adding imperceptible perturbations, attackers can trick AI systems into making incorrect decisions or misclassifying objects.

Adversarial attacks pose a significant challenge in security-critical applications, such as autonomous vehicles or facial recognition systems. For example, an attacker can place stickers on a stop sign that are imperceptible to humans but cause an autonomous vehicle to misinterpret the sign as a speed limit sign. Similarly, in facial recognition systems, adversarial attacks can be used to manipulate images or wear specially crafted patterns that can fool the system into misidentifying individuals.

These attacks exploit the vulnerabilities and limitations of AI models, revealing their susceptibility to small changes in input data. Adversarial attacks highlight the need for robustness and resilience in AI systems, as well as the importance of evaluating and hardening models against such attacks.

Researchers are actively exploring defense mechanisms to mitigate the impact of adversarial attacks. Techniques such as adversarial training, where models are exposed to adversarial examples during the training process, and defensive distillation, which involves training models to be resistant to adversarial examples, have shown promising results. However, achieving robustness against adversarial attacks remains an ongoing challenge in AI research.

5.2.5 Lack of Contextual Understanding and Emotional Intelligence

AI systems often struggle with understanding context and emotional intelligence, which can limit their decision-making capabilities, particularly in natural language processing tasks. While AI models can generate coherent and grammatically correct sentences, they often lack a deeper understanding of the meaning and emotional nuances conveyed in human language.

Understanding context is essential for accurate interpretation and decision-making in natural language understanding tasks. For example, a chatbot responding to customer queries needs to understand the context of the conversation to provide relevant and helpful responses. Without context, the AI system may misinterpret user queries or provide generic and irrelevant answers.

Similarly, emotional intelligence is crucial for effective communication and decision-making in human interactions. AI systems that lack emotional intelligence can struggle to recognize and respond appropriately to emotions expressed by users. This limitation can lead to insensitive or inappropriate responses, especially in applications such as mental health support or customer service, where empathy and emotional understanding are paramount.

Addressing the lack of contextual understanding and emotional intelligence in AI systems is a complex task. It requires advancements in natural language processing and sentiment analysis, as well as the development of models that can interpret and respond to the emotional cues embedded in human language.

Researchers are exploring various approaches to improve contextual understanding and emotional intelligence in AI systems. This includes incorporating contextual information from previous conversations, leveraging external knowledge sources, and integrating sentiment analysis techniques to infer the emotional state of users. Additionally, efforts are being made to develop AI models that can generate responses that are not only grammatically correct but also contextually relevant and emotionally appropriate.

However, achieving a comprehensive understanding of context and emotional intelligence in AI systems is still a significant challenge. Human language is complex, nuanced, and heavily influenced by cultural and social factors, making it difficult for AI models to capture and interpret all its subtleties accurately.

5.2.6 Overreliance on Training Data and Generalization

AI systems heavily rely on the training data they are exposed to, and their decision-making is based on patterns and correlations learned from that data. However, this overreliance on training data can lead to limitations in decision-making when faced with situations or data that deviate from the training distribution.

When an AI system encounters data that is significantly different from what it was trained on, it may struggle to make accurate decisions. This phenomenon, known as distributional shift, can occur due to changes in the real-world environment, novel scenarios, or unseen variations in the input data. For example, an autonomous driving system trained on data collected during daylight may have difficulty operating in low-light conditions or during heavy rain.

Generalization is a key aspect of AI decision-making, as it allows models to apply their learned knowledge to unseen examples. However, the ability of AI systems to generalize well depends on the quality, diversity, and representativeness of the training data. If the training data is limited or biased, or if the data used for evaluation differs significantly from the training data, the AI system's ability to generalize accurately can be compromised.

Improving the generalization capabilities of AI systems requires addressing issues such as data bias, dataset imbalance, and ensuring that the training data covers a wide range of scenarios and variations. Techniques such as data augmentation, transfer learning, and domain adaptation can help mitigate the limitations caused by overreliance on training data and improve the generalization performance of AI models.

Additionally, ongoing monitoring and evaluation of AI systems in real-world applications are crucial to detect and address limitations in decision-making due to distributional shift. Continuous learning and updating of models based on feedback and new data can help adapt AI systems to evolving environments and improve their decision-making capabilities.

5.2.7 Ethical Considerations and Accountability

The limitations and biases in AI decision-making raise significant ethical considerations and the need for accountability. AI systems have the potential to impact individuals and societies in various ways, and decisions made by these systems can have far-reaching consequences.

When AI systems make biased decisions or perpetuate existing biases in society, they can contribute to unfairness, discrimination, and marginalization of certain groups. This not only violates ethical principles but also raises legal and regulatory concerns, particularly in areas such as healthcare, finance, and criminal justice.

Ensuring accountability in AI decision-making is challenging due to the complex nature of AI systems and the involvement of multiple stakeholders. Developers, policymakers, and organizations deploying AI systems have a responsibility to address the limitations and biases in decision-making and take steps to mitigate their impact.

Transparency and explainability play a crucial role in fostering accountability.

5.3 Impact on Human Creativity and Innovation

Artificial Intelligence (AI) has made significant advancements in recent years and has permeated various aspects of human life, including industries, healthcare, transportation, and entertainment. However, along with its benefits, AI systems also have biases and limitations that can impact human creativity and innovation. In this essay, we will explore the ways in which bias and limitations in AI systems affect human creativity and innovation, and discuss potential solutions to mitigate these issues.

Bias in AI Systems

Bias in AI systems refers to the systematic favoritism or discrimination towards certain groups or individuals. These biases can arise from various sources, such as biased training data, biased algorithms, or biased decision-making processes.

When AI systems exhibit bias, they can perpetuate existing social, cultural, and gender inequalities, thereby limiting the potential for creativity and innovation.

1.1 Social Bias

AI systems are trained on vast amounts of data, and if the training data is biased, the AI system can learn and perpetuate those biases. For example, if a facial recognition system is trained predominantly on data of lighter-skinned individuals, it may struggle to accurately recognize and classify faces of people with darker skin tones. This can lead to misidentification, exclusion, and discrimination, affecting the participation of diverse individuals in creative and innovative activities.

1.2 Cultural Bias

Cultural biases can also be present in AI systems, particularly in natural language processing (NLP) algorithms. Language models trained on text data from specific cultures or regions may inadvertently reflect the biases present in that data. For instance, if an AI system is trained on a dataset containing predominantly male-authored literature, it may exhibit biases in generating text that aligns with traditional gender roles, limiting the scope of creative and innovative outputs.

1.3 Gender Bias

Gender bias is another significant concern in AI systems. Studies have shown that AI algorithms can exhibit gender bias, for example, by associating certain professions or roles more strongly with a specific gender. Such biases can reinforce existing stereotypes and hinder opportunities for women and other gender minorities to engage in creative and innovative endeavors, limiting the diversity of ideas and perspectives.

Limitations in AI Systems

In addition to biases, AI systems have inherent limitations that can impact human creativity and innovation. These limitations arise from factors such as data availability, algorithmic constraints, and the inability of AI systems to understand complex human emotions and context.

2.1 Data Limitations

AI systems heavily rely on data for training and decision-making. However, limitations in data availability can hinder the creativity and innovation potential of AI systems. For instance, if an AI system is trained on a limited dataset that does not capture the full range of human experiences, it may struggle to generate diverse and novel ideas. Furthermore, data limitations can lead to underrepresentation of certain demographics or domains, resulting in biased outcomes and stifling innovation.

2.2 Algorithmic Constraints

AI algorithms are designed to optimize specific objectives based on the training data. While they excel at pattern recognition and optimization tasks, they may lack the flexibility and contextual understanding that humans possess. This can limit the ability of AI systems to think creatively or generate innovative solutions to complex problems that require a deep understanding of context, nuance, and subjective judgment.

2.3 Lack of Emotional and Contextual Understanding

Human creativity and innovation often stem from emotions, intuition, and a nuanced understanding of social and cultural contexts. However, AI systems currently lack the ability to fully comprehend and respond to complex emotions and contextual cues. This limitation hampers their capacity to generate creative ideas or innovative solutions that resonate with human experiences, emotions, and values.

Impact on Human Creativity and Innovation

The biases and limitations in AI systems can have several detrimental effects on human creativity and innovation.

3.1 Reduction in Diversity of Ideas

Bias in AI systems can lead to a reduction in the diversity of ideas. When AI systems perpetuate existing biases, they reinforce the dominant narratives and perspectives present in the training data. This can result in a narrower range of ideas being generated or recommended by AI systems, limiting the exploration of alternative viewpoints and hindering the emergence of innovative and groundbreaking ideas. Creativity thrives on diversity and the collision of different perspectives, and bias in AI systems can impede this process.

3.2 Reinforcement of Stereotypes

AI systems that exhibit biases can reinforce stereotypes, thereby inhibiting the ability to challenge societal norms and preconceptions. For example, if an AI-powered recommendation system consistently suggests certain types of content or products based on biased data, it can perpetuate stereotypes and limit individuals' exposure to new and diverse ideas. This can hinder the exploration of unconventional approaches and novel ideas, hampering creativity and innovation.

3.3 Exclusion of Underrepresented Groups

Biased AI systems can lead to the exclusion of underrepresented groups from participating in creative and innovative activities. When AI algorithms are biased against certain demographics, these groups may face barriers to access and opportunities. For instance, if an AI-powered hiring system is biased against female candidates, it can perpetuate gender disparities and hinder the inclusion of diverse perspectives in innovative teams. This exclusion limits the pool of talent and diversity of ideas, ultimately stifling creativity and innovation.

3.4 Reduced Human-AI Collaboration

Limitations in AI systems, such as their inability to understand complex emotions and contexts, can hinder effective collaboration between humans and AI. Human creativity often arises from the combination of emotional intelligence, intuition, and analytical thinking. When AI systems are unable to comprehend and respond to these human qualities, the potential for synergistic collaborations and the emergence of innovative ideas may be diminished. Human-AI collaboration has the potential to unlock new creative possibilities and drive innovation, but it requires AI systems to be more capable of understanding and engaging with human nuances.

Mitigating Bias and Limitations

Addressing bias and limitations in AI systems is crucial to fostering human creativity and innovation. Several strategies can be employed to mitigate these issues:

4.1 Diverse and Representative Training Data

Ensuring that AI systems are trained on diverse and representative datasets is essential to reduce bias. Data collection efforts should prioritize inclusivity, encompassing a wide range of demographics, cultures, and perspectives. Additionally, it is important to regularly audit and update training data to account for changing societal norms and evolving perspectives.

4.2 Algorithmic Fairness and Transparency

Developers should prioritize algorithmic fairness and transparency when designing AI systems. This includes conducting rigorous testing and evaluation to identify and rectify biases in algorithms.

Employing techniques such as algorithmic auditing, fairness-aware learning, and interpretability can help uncover and address bias. Making AI systems transparent and explainable can enhance trust and enable users to understand and challenge the system's decisions.

4.3 Ethical Guidelines and Regulations

The development and deployment of AI systems should be guided by ethical guidelines and regulations that explicitly address bias and limitations. Governments, organizations, and research institutions should collaborate to establish frameworks that promote fairness, accountability, and transparency in AI systems. This can include guidelines for data collection, algorithm development, and bias mitigation strategies.

4.4 Human-in-the-Loop Approach

Adopting a human-in-the-loop approach can help mitigate the limitations of AI systems. By involving humans in the decision-making process, AI outputs can be validated, corrected, and complemented with human expertise. This approach acknowledges that humans possess unique creative and intuitive capabilities that can enhance the outputs of AI systems.

4.5 Continuous Evaluation and Improvement

AI systems should be subject to continuous evaluation and improvement to ensure ongoing mitigation of biases and limitations. Regular audits, user feedback, and performance monitoring can help identify and address any emerging biases or limitations. This process should be iterative, with regular updates and refinements to the algorithms and models based on the feedback and insights gained from real-world usage.

4.6 Interdisciplinary Collaboration

Promoting interdisciplinary collaboration between experts in AI, social sciences, humanities, and ethics can contribute to addressing bias and limitations in AI systems. By bringing together diverse perspectives, knowledge, and expertise, it is possible to develop more robust and inclusive AI systems that better account for human creativity, cultural nuances, and ethical considerations.

Promoting Human Creativity and Innovation in AI Systems

While bias and limitations in AI systems can have negative impacts on human creativity and innovation, there are also opportunities to leverage AI to enhance and foster these qualities. By addressing bias and limitations, AI systems can be designed to augment human creativity and innovation rather than stifling them. Here are a few ways in which AI can contribute positively:

5.1 Data-driven Inspiration

AI systems can analyze vast amounts of data from diverse sources, uncovering patterns and insights that may not be immediately apparent to humans. This data-driven inspiration can fuel creative thinking and provide novel perspectives to human creators and innovators. AI-powered recommendation systems, content generation tools, and trend analysis algorithms can offer valuable insights and inspiration for creative endeavors.

5.2 Collaborative AI Tools

AI systems can serve as collaborative tools that work in tandem with human creators and innovators. For example, AI-powered design tools can assist in generating and refining visual designs, while natural language processing algorithms can help writers with language suggestions and editing. Such collaborative tools can leverage the strengths of AI systems while incorporating human creativity and intuition to produce innovative outputs.

5.3 Personalized and Adaptive Support

AI systems can provide personalized and adaptive support to individuals engaged in creative and innovative activities. By analyzing user preferences, behavior, and past work, AI can offer tailored recommendations, feedback, and suggestions that align with the individual's creative goals. This personalized support can enhance productivity, inspire new ideas, and enable individuals to push the boundaries of their creativity.

5.4 Automation of Repetitive Tasks

AI systems can automate repetitive and mundane tasks, freeing up time and mental energy for human creators and innovators to focus on higher-level thinking and ideation. By taking care of routine tasks such as data analysis, image processing, or administrative work, AI allows individuals to invest more time and energy in exploring innovative ideas and pushing the boundaries of creativity.

5.5 Enhanced Access to Knowledge and Resources

AI systems can improve access to knowledge and resources, democratizing the creative and innovative process. Through AI-powered search engines, recommendation systems, and online platforms, individuals can discover a wide range of information, tools, and opportunities for creative exploration. This expanded access can unlock new possibilities and facilitate collaboration among diverse individuals, promoting innovation and creativity.

Bias and limitations in AI systems have significant implications for human creativity and innovation. Biased AI systems can perpetuate inequalities, reinforce stereotypes, and exclude underrepresented groups, while limitations in AI's contextual understanding and emotional intelligence can hinder collaboration and the generation of novel ideas. However, through proactive efforts to mitigate bias, enhance transparency, and foster interdisciplinary collaboration, it is possible to develop AI systems that augment and support human creativity and innovation. By leveraging AI's strengths, such as data-driven inspiration, collaborative tools, personalized support, and automation of repetitive tasks, we can create a more inclusive and empowering environment for human creativity and innovation in the era of AI.

Dependency on AI Technology
6.1 Automation and Job Displacement

In recent years, artificial intelligence (AI) technology has made significant strides, revolutionizing various industries and transforming the way we live and work. AI systems are capable of performing complex tasks, making decisions, and even mimicking human intelligence to some extent. While AI technology brings numerous benefits and advancements, it also raises concerns about the potential displacement of jobs and the implications for the workforce. This article explores the relationship between automation, job displacement, and the growing dependency on AI technology.

Understanding Automation:

Automation refers to the use of technology, including AI systems, to perform tasks that were previously carried out by humans. Automation has been a part of human history since the industrial revolution, with machines taking over repetitive and labor-intensive tasks. However, the advent of AI has significantly expanded the scope and capabilities of automation. AI systems can analyze vast amounts of data, recognize patterns, and make predictions, enabling them to perform tasks that were once exclusively within the domain of human intelligence.

AI and Job Displacement:

One of the primary concerns surrounding AI technology is its potential to displace human workers. As AI systems become more advanced, they are increasingly capable of replacing humans in a wide range of jobs. Tasks that require repetitive actions, data analysis, or rule-based decision-making can be automated using AI algorithms. This automation can lead to a decrease in the demand for human labor, resulting in job displacement.

Several sectors are particularly vulnerable to job displacement due to AI technology. For example, manufacturing industries have been implementing robotic systems for years, replacing human workers on assembly lines. Similarly, customer service and call centers have started using AI-powered chatbots and virtual assistants to handle customer inquiries, reducing the need for human operators. In the transportation industry, self-driving vehicles threaten the jobs of professional drivers, and in the financial sector, AI algorithms can perform tasks traditionally done by human analysts and traders.

While the extent of job displacement varies across industries, the potential impact on the workforce is significant. According to a report by McKinsey Global Institute, by 2030, between 400 million and 800 million workers could be displaced globally due to automation, representing approximately one-fifth of the global workforce. The report also suggests that the impact will be uneven, affecting certain occupations and industries more severely than others.

Challenges and Concerns:

The displacement of jobs due to AI technology presents several challenges and concerns for individuals, communities, and society as a whole. Some of the key challenges and concerns include:

Unemployment and Income Inequality: Job displacement can lead to unemployment, creating financial hardships for individuals and their families. Additionally, the loss of jobs can contribute to income inequality, as those who possess the skills to work alongside AI systems may benefit, while others face difficulties finding new employment opportunities.

Skill Mismatch: The rapid advancement of AI technology may outpace the ability of workers to acquire the necessary skills for new jobs. As AI systems automate routine tasks, the demand for workers with specialized skills in areas such as data analysis, programming, and AI development increases. This can create a skill mismatch, where the supply of workers with relevant skills does not meet the demand, further exacerbating unemployment and income inequality.

Psychological and Societal Impact: Job displacement can have profound psychological effects on individuals. Losing a job can lead to feelings of insecurity, anxiety, and a loss of identity. Communities that heavily rely on industries susceptible to automation may experience social and economic disruption, contributing to social unrest and dislocation.

Retraining and Reskilling: To mitigate the negative impacts of job displacement, retraining and reskilling programs become crucial. However, implementing effective retraining initiatives at scale poses significant challenges. It requires substantial investment in education and training infrastructure, coordination between governments and educational institutions, and the willingness of individuals to adapt to new skill sets. Furthermore, retraining programs need to be agile and responsive to the evolving demands of the job market to ensure that displaced workers can acquire relevant skills and find new employment opportunities.

Addressing the Challenges:

While the challenges posed by job displacement due to AI technology are significant, there are steps that individuals, organizations, and governments can take to mitigate the negative impacts and foster a smoother transition. Some potential strategies include:

Lifelong Learning: Encouraging a culture of lifelong learning is essential to equip individuals with the skills needed to adapt to the changing job market. This involves promoting continuous education and upskilling opportunities for workers throughout their careers. Employers can play a crucial role by investing in training programs and providing resources for employees to acquire new skills and stay relevant in the age of AI.

Collaboration between Industry and Academia: Close collaboration between industry and academia is vital to ensure that educational institutions are producing graduates with the skills required by the job market. This collaboration can take the form of curriculum development, internships, apprenticeships, and joint research projects. By aligning education with industry needs, it becomes easier for individuals to acquire the skills that are in demand.

Social Safety Nets: Governments and policymakers must design and implement robust social safety nets to support individuals who face job displacement. This can include unemployment benefits, job placement services, and income support programs. Furthermore, efforts should be made to provide affordable healthcare, housing, and other essential services to individuals during their transition period.

Entrepreneurship and Innovation: Encouraging entrepreneurship and supporting innovation can create new opportunities for job creation. Governments can provide incentives, funding, and mentorship programs to foster a thriving startup ecosystem. Entrepreneurship enables individuals to harness their skills and knowledge to create new ventures and adapt to the changing economic landscape.

Ethical AI Deployment: As AI technology continues to advance, it is crucial to ensure its ethical and responsible deployment. This includes addressing biases in AI algorithms, maintaining transparency, and considering the social and ethical implications of AI systems. By adhering to ethical guidelines, the potential negative impacts of AI on jobs and society can be mitigated.

Job Transition Support: Implementing effective job transition support programs can assist displaced workers in finding new employment opportunities. This can involve providing career counseling, job search assistance, and facilitating networking opportunities. Additionally, financial support for relocation and retraining expenses can ease the transition process for individuals.

Redefining Work and Job Roles: As certain tasks become automated, it provides an opportunity to redefine work and job roles. Instead of fearing job displacement, individuals can focus on acquiring skills that complement AI technology. This may involve developing creative and critical thinking abilities, emotional intelligence, and other uniquely human skills that are difficult to automate.

The dependency on AI technology has undoubtedly led to increased automation and job displacement.

While the full extent of the impact remains uncertain, it is crucial to acknowledge the challenges and concerns associated with this trend. By addressing these challenges proactively, through a combination of education, collaboration, support systems, and ethical practices, it is possible to mitigate the negative impacts of job displacement and foster a future where humans and AI technology coexist harmoniously. It is essential to view AI technology as a tool that complements human capabilities rather than a replacement for human workers, and to strive for a society where the benefits of AI are shared equitably among all members.

Reduced Need for Memory and Recall

In today's fast-paced world, the rapid advancement of AI technology has brought about significant changes in various aspects of our lives. One area where AI has had a profound impact is in reducing the need for human memory and recall. With the availability of smart devices, virtual assistants, and AI-powered applications, individuals now rely heavily on AI to store and retrieve information on their behalf. While this dependency on AI technology offers convenience and efficiency, it also raises concerns about the potential consequences and drawbacks associated with reduced reliance on human memory and recall.

Memory and recall are fundamental cognitive functions that enable us to acquire, store, and retrieve information. They play a crucial role in our everyday lives, allowing us to learn new things, make decisions based on past experiences, and engage in complex problem-solving tasks. However, as AI technology evolves, it increasingly assumes the role of a cognitive assistant, taking over some of the tasks traditionally performed by human memory.

One of the primary ways in which AI reduces the need for memory and recall is through data storage and retrieval. In the past, individuals relied on their memory to retain information such as phone numbers, addresses, and important dates. Today, with the widespread use of smartphones and digital calendars, AI-powered applications automatically store and organize this information for us. This shift has undoubtedly made life more convenient, freeing up mental resources that were previously dedicated to remembering mundane details.

Furthermore, virtual assistants such as Siri, Google Assistant, and Alexa have become ubiquitous in many households. These AI-powered agents can answer questions, provide recommendations, and perform various tasks on command. Their ability to access vast amounts of information within seconds reduces the need for individuals to rely on their memory to recall specific facts or figures. Instead, they can simply ask their virtual assistant for the desired information, allowing them to offload the cognitive burden onto AI technology.

AI technology has also made significant strides in automating routine tasks and decision-making processes. For example, email filters can now sort incoming messages based on priority or relevance, eliminating the need for users to manually sift through their inbox. Similarly, AI algorithms can analyze large datasets and provide insights, reducing the cognitive effort required to make informed decisions. These advancements have undoubtedly increased efficiency and productivity, but they also contribute to a reduced reliance on human memory and recall.

While the benefits of reduced dependency on memory and recall are evident, there are also potential drawbacks and concerns that arise from this reliance on AI technology. One major concern is the potential erosion of human cognitive abilities. Just as physical fitness requires regular exercise to maintain optimal health, cognitive abilities, including memory and recall, also require practice and use to stay sharp. When individuals rely heavily on AI to perform cognitive tasks, they may experience a decline in their own cognitive abilities over time.

Additionally, there is the risk of over-reliance on AI systems that are not infallible. AI technology, despite its remarkable advancements, is still prone to errors and limitations. It relies on algorithms and data inputs, which can introduce biases or inaccuracies. When individuals excessively depend on AI for information recall or decision-making, they may overlook potential errors or blindly trust the AI system's output without critical evaluation.

This blind trust can lead to misinformation or poor decision-making, especially when dealing with complex or sensitive matters.

Another concern is the potential loss of personal and cultural knowledge. Human memory is not just a storage mechanism; it is also intertwined with our personal experiences, emotions, and cultural heritage. Our memories shape our identities and help us form connections with others. When we rely on AI systems to store and retrieve our memories, we risk losing the personal touch and emotional depth associated with those memories. AI technology lacks the ability to understand the subjective nuances and emotional significance that make our memories unique and meaningful.

Furthermore, the reliance on AI Furthermore, the reliance on AI for memory and recall raises concerns about privacy and data security. When individuals entrust their personal information, memories, and preferences to AI systems, they expose themselves to potential privacy breaches and data misuse. AI algorithms are designed to learn from user data and behavior patterns, which can raise ethical questions about the ownership and control of personal information. There have been instances where AI systems have been compromised or hacked, leading to the unauthorized access and exposure of sensitive data. Therefore, the more we depend on AI for memory and recall, the greater the need for robust security measures to protect our personal information.

Additionally, the reduced need for memory and recall may have unintended consequences for our cognitive abilities and overall well-being. Memory and recall are cognitive processes that exercise our brain and promote mental agility. When we rely on AI to store and retrieve information on our behalf, we may inadvertently limit our brain's opportunities for exercise and growth. This lack of mental stimulation can potentially lead to cognitive decline, decreased attention span, and reduced critical thinking skills. It is essential to strike a balance between utilizing AI technology for convenience while still actively engaging our memory and recall abilities to maintain cognitive health.

Another significant concern related to the reduced need for memory and recall is the potential loss of human creativity and innovation. Memory and recall are not just about retaining and retrieving information; they also contribute to the formation of new ideas and insights. Our ability to connect different pieces of information stored in our memory is crucial for problem-solving, innovation, and creativity. When we overly rely on AI for information recall, we may miss out on the serendipitous connections and unique perspectives that human memory can provide. Human memory has a context-dependent nature, allowing us to draw on past experiences and knowledge to generate novel solutions. By solely depending on AI for memory and recall, we may limit our capacity for originality and ingenuity.

To mitigate the potential negative impacts of reduced reliance on human memory and recall, it is crucial to foster a balanced approach that leverages AI technology while still maintaining and nurturing our cognitive abilities. Here are a few strategies to consider:

Practice Active Engagement: Despite the convenience of AI technology, it is essential to actively engage our memory and recall abilities. Engage in activities that challenge your memory, such as puzzles, brain games, or learning new skills. By actively exercising our cognitive abilities, we can help maintain and improve them over time.

Critical Evaluation of AI Outputs: While AI systems can provide quick access to information, it is important to critically evaluate their outputs. Be aware of the limitations and potential biases of AI algorithms. Cross-reference information from multiple sources to ensure accuracy and avoid blindly accepting AI-generated information.

Maintain a Personal Memory Repository: While AI can assist in storing and organizing information, it is still valuable to maintain a personal memory repository. Keep journals, photo albums, or other physical or digital artifacts that capture personal experiences and memories. These tangible reminders can help preserve the emotional depth and personal connections associated with our memories.

Strengthen Data Security: Given the potential privacy risks associated with AI technology, prioritize data security measures. Regularly review privacy settings on AI-powered devices and applications. Be cautious about the type and amount of personal information shared with AI systems and ensure that robust security measures are in place to protect sensitive data.

Embrace Human Creativity: While AI can provide efficient information recall, remember that human creativity and innovation are irreplaceable. Embrace activities that foster creativity, such as art, music, writing, or problem-solving tasks that require thinking outside the box. By nurturing our creative abilities, we can tap into the unique strengths of the human mind.

6.3 Effects on Social Interaction and Communication

The rapid advancement of artificial intelligence (AI) technology has brought about significant changes in various aspects of our lives, including social interaction and communication. AI-powered systems and applications have become ubiquitous, influencing how we connect, communicate, and interact with others. While AI technology offers numerous benefits and conveniences, it also poses certain challenges and concerns regarding its impact on social interaction and communication. This essay will explore the effects of AI technology on social interaction and communication, examining both the positive and negative aspects of this dependency.

Enhanced Communication Efficiency

One of the most notable positive effects of AI technology on social interaction and communication is the significant enhancement of communication efficiency. AI-powered communication platforms and applications, such as chatbots and virtual assistants, have revolutionized the way we interact with businesses, organizations, and even with each other. These systems employ natural language processing and machine learning algorithms to understand and respond to user queries and requests.

For instance, virtual assistants like Siri, Alexa, and Google Assistant have become integrated into our daily lives, providing quick and accurate responses to our inquiries, managing our schedules, and even controlling our smart homes. This increased efficiency in communication allows individuals to save time and effort, enabling them to focus on other important tasks. Moreover, AI-powered translation tools have facilitated cross-cultural communication, breaking down language barriers and fostering global connections.

Additionally, social media platforms employ AI algorithms to personalize and optimize users' feeds, suggesting relevant content and connections. These algorithms analyze user preferences, behaviors, and interactions to deliver tailored experiences, fostering more meaningful and engaging interactions. This personalized communication experience enables individuals to connect with like-minded people, discover relevant information, and build communities of shared interests.

Improved Accessibility for Individuals with Disabilities

AI technology has also played a significant role in improving accessibility for individuals with disabilities, thus enhancing their social interaction and communication. AI-powered assistive technologies have transformed the lives of people with visual, auditory, or physical impairments, enabling them to communicate effectively and participate more fully in society.

For example, speech recognition technology, coupled with natural language processing algorithms, has made it possible for individuals with mobility impairments to control devices and communicate through voice commands. Moreover, AI-driven image recognition and text-to-speech systems have allowed individuals with visual impairments to access and interact with digital content, including social media platforms, emails, and online articles.

Such advancements in AI technology have empowered individuals with disabilities, enabling them to express themselves, connect with others, and engage in social interactions more independently. Consequently, AI has facilitated a more inclusive society where everyone can participate and communicate on equal terms.

Concerns of Dehumanization

While AI technology has undoubtedly improved communication efficiency and accessibility, there are concerns regarding its potential dehumanizing effects on social interaction and communication. With the increasing reliance on AI-powered systems, there is a risk of diminishing the authenticity and personal touch that are inherent in human communication.

For instance, the use of chatbots and virtual assistants in customer service interactions has raised concerns about the loss of human connection. While these AI systems can provide quick and efficient responses, they may lack the empathy and emotional understanding that human customer service agents can offer. The absence of genuine human interaction can leave individuals feeling dissatisfied or detached, especially in situations that require empathy and emotional support.

Similarly, the personalization algorithms used by social media platforms may inadvertently contribute to the creation of echo chambers and filter bubbles. These algorithms prioritize content that aligns with users' preferences, beliefs, and behaviors, resulting in a limited exposure to diverse perspectives and opinions. As a consequence, individuals may find themselves surrounded by like-minded individuals, reinforcing existing beliefs and contributing to the polarization of society.

Moreover, the proliferation of AI-generated deep fakes, which are realistic but manipulated audio or video recordings, poses a significant threat to privacy and trust in communication. Deepfakes can be used to deceive and manipulate individuals by making it difficult to discern between genuine and manipulated content. This can lead to the erosion of trust in communication channels, as people become skeptical about the authenticity of the information they receive.

Impact on Interpersonal Relationships

AI technology's influence on social interaction and communication extends to interpersonal relationships, both online and offline. While AI-powered communication tools have made it easier to connect with others, there are concerns about the potential impact on the quality and depth of these relationships.

In the digital era, individuals often rely on social media platforms and messaging applications as the primary means of communication. While these platforms facilitate instant and convenient interactions, they can also contribute to a sense of superficiality and shallow connections. Communication mediated by AI algorithms may lack the nuances and non-verbal cues that are present in face-to-face interactions, making it challenging to fully understand and empathize with others.

Furthermore, the constant exposure to curated and idealized versions of people's lives on social media platforms can lead to social comparison and feelings of inadequacy. The pressure to present oneself in a favorable light and gain social validation can negatively impact self-esteem and create a barrier to genuine and authentic communication.

Additionally, the advent of AI-powered dating applications has changed the landscape of romantic relationships. While these apps offer convenience and efficiency in finding potential partners, they also introduce a gamified approach to dating, where individuals are reduced to profiles and algorithms. This can undermine the natural and organic process of building relationships, focusing more on superficial attributes rather than genuine compatibility.

Ethical Considerations and Bias

Another aspect of AI technology's impact on social interaction and communication is the ethical considerations and potential biases associated with AI algorithms. AI systems learn from vast amounts of data, and if the training data contains biases or discriminatory patterns, the algorithms can perpetuate and amplify those biases.

This raises concerns regarding fairness, equity, and inclusivity in communication. Biased algorithms can lead to discriminatory outcomes in various contexts, such as job applications, content moderation, and targeted advertising. These biases can exacerbate existing social inequalities and further marginalize certain groups of individuals.

Moreover, the collection and analysis of personal data by AI systems for targeted advertising and content personalization raise concerns about privacy and data protection. AI algorithms have access to vast amounts of personal information, which can be used for manipulative purposes or unauthorized surveillance. This can undermine individuals' trust in communication platforms and compromise their privacy.

Mitigating the Negative Effects

To mitigate the negative effects of AI technology on social interaction and communication, several measures can be taken:

Human-Centered Design: When developing AI-powered communication systems, a human-centered design approach should be adopted. This involves considering the user's needs, preferences, and emotions, ensuring that AI technology enhances rather than replaces human interaction.

Transparency and Accountability: AI algorithms should be transparent, with clear explanations of how they make decisions. Ethical guidelines and standards should be established to ensure fairness, prevent discrimination, and address biases in AI systems.

Enhanced Digital Literacy: Promoting digital literacy and critical thinking skills can empower individuals to navigate and understand AI-mediated communication effectively. This includes educating users about the limitations and potential risks of AI technology, enabling them to make informed decisions.

Striking a Balance: While AI technology offers convenience and efficiency, it is essential to strike a balance between AI-mediated communication and face-to-face interactions. Encouraging offline social interactions and maintaining strong interpersonal relationships can help preserve the authenticity and depth of human connections.

Ethical Data Use: Organizations and platforms utilizing AI technology should prioritize privacy and data protection. Implementing robust security measures, obtaining informed consent for data collection, and providing individuals with control over their personal information can help build trust and ensure responsible data Regular Auditing and Regulation: Regular audits of AI algorithms and systems should be conducted to identify and rectify biases, discrimination, and privacy concerns. Governments and regulatory bodies should establish clear guidelines and regulations for the ethical use of AI technology in social interaction and communication.

User Empowerment: Empowering users with control over their AI-mediated interactions can enhance their autonomy and agency. Providing users with options to customize their AI experiences, opt-out of certain AI features, and choose the level of personalization can give individuals a sense of control and ownership over their communication.

Continued Research and Collaboration: Ongoing research and collaboration among interdisciplinary fields, including computer science, psychology, sociology, and ethics, can contribute to a deeper understanding of the effects of AI on social interaction and communication. This collaboration can lead to the development of AI systems that are more aligned with human needs and values.

The dependency on AI technology in social interaction and communication brings both benefits and challenges. AI has significantly enhanced communication efficiency, improved accessibility for individuals with disabilities, and facilitated global connections. However, concerns regarding dehumanization, impact on interpersonal relationships, ethical considerations, and biases remain.

To ensure the responsible and positive use of AI technology in social interaction and communication, it is crucial to adopt a human-centered approach, promote transparency and accountability, enhance digital literacy, strike a balance between AI-mediated and face-to-face interactions, prioritize ethical data use, conduct regular audits, and empower users. Through these efforts, we can harness the potential of AI while preserving the authenticity, depth, and inclusivity of human communication in the digital age.

7.1 Privacy and Data Security Concerns

In today's digital age, privacy and data security concerns have become increasingly prevalent. With the rapid advancements in technology and the widespread collection and use of personal data, ethical considerations surrounding privacy and data security have become a critical issue. This essay will explore the ethical challenges and considerations related to privacy and data security, examining the potential risks and the responsibility of various stakeholders in safeguarding individuals' privacy.

Understanding Privacy and Data Security

Privacy refers to the right of individuals to control and protect their personal information and the freedom to decide how their data is collected, used, and shared. Data security, on the other hand, focuses on protecting data from unauthorized access, disclosure, alteration, or destruction.

Privacy and data security are closely intertwined, as effective data security measures are essential for safeguarding individuals' privacy.

Privacy and data security concerns arise due to several factors, including the widespread collection and storage of personal data, the increasing use of data analytics and profiling techniques, and the potential for data breaches or unauthorized access to sensitive information. Ethical considerations come into play when determining how personal data should be handled, who should have access to it, and the extent to which individuals' privacy should be respected.

Risks to Privacy and Data Security

There are various risks associated with privacy and data security that can have significant ethical implications. Some of the key risks include:

Data Breaches: Data breaches occur when unauthorized individuals gain access to sensitive data. These breaches can result in significant harm to individuals, such as identity theft, financial loss, or reputational damage. The responsibility to protect personal data falls on the organizations collecting and storing it, and they must take adequate measures to prevent data breaches.

Profiling and Discrimination: The extensive collection and analysis of personal data enable profiling, which involves the categorization and segmentation of individuals based on their characteristics or behavior. While profiling can have benefits, such as targeted advertising or personalized recommendations, it also raises concerns about discrimination and unfair treatment. Ethical considerations involve ensuring that profiling practices are transparent, unbiased, and respectful of individuals' rights.

Surveillance and Government Intrusion: With the advancement of surveillance technologies, governments and other entities have the potential to monitor individuals' activities and collect vast amounts of personal data. The ethical challenge lies in finding the right balance between ensuring national security and protecting individuals' privacy rights. Governments should have clear legal frameworks and oversight mechanisms to prevent abuse of surveillance powers and ensure transparency and accountability.

Consent and Control: Individuals should have control over their personal data and the ability to give informed consent regarding its collection and use. However, in practice, individuals often face challenges in understanding complex privacy policies and making meaningful choices about data sharing. Ethical considerations involve promoting clear and accessible privacy policies, providing meaningful consent mechanisms, and empowering individuals to exercise control over their data.

Stakeholders and their Responsibilities

Ensuring privacy and data security is a shared responsibility among various stakeholders, including individuals, organizations, governments, and technology providers. Each stakeholder has a role to play in addressing the ethical challenges associated with privacy and data security.

Individuals: Individuals have a responsibility to be aware of the privacy risks associated with sharing their personal data and to make informed choices about data disclosure. It is important for individuals to educate themselves about privacy settings, read privacy policies, and exercise caution when sharing personal information online. By being mindful of their digital footprint, individuals can contribute to protecting their own privacy.

Organizations: Organizations that collect and use personal data have an ethical duty to prioritize privacy and data security. This includes implementing robust security measures to protect data, being transparent about data practices, and obtaining informed consent from individuals. Organizations should also establish clear data retention policies and ensure that data is not used for purposes beyond what was initially disclosed or consented to.

Governments

Governments: Governments play a crucial role in developing and enforcing regulations and policies that protect privacy and data security. They should establish legal frameworks that define the rights and responsibilities of individuals and organizations regarding data protection. Governments should also promote awareness and education about privacy rights and ensure effective oversight and enforcement mechanisms to hold organizations accountable for privacy violations. Additionally, governments have a responsibility to strike a balance between surveillance and privacy, ensuring that surveillance activities are necessary, proportionate, and conducted within legal boundaries.

Technology Providers: Technology providers, including software developers, social media platforms, and data analytics companies, have an ethical responsibility to design and develop technologies with privacy and data security in mind. They should implement privacy-by-design principles, which involve incorporating privacy considerations into every stage of technology development. This includes providing clear privacy settings, offering strong data encryption, and minimizing data collection and retention.

Ethical Considerations and Solutions

Addressing privacy and data security concerns requires careful ethical deliberation and the implementation of appropriate solutions. Some of the ethical considerations and potential solutions include:

Transparency and Accountability: Organizations should be transparent about their data collection and use practices. They should provide clear and accessible privacy policies, inform individuals about the purposes and scope of data collection, and ensure that individuals have meaningful choices and control over their data. Organizations should also establish mechanisms for individuals to access, correct, or delete their data and provide avenues for redress in case of privacy violations.

Minimization and Purpose Limitation: Organizations should collect and retain only the minimum amount of personal data necessary for the intended purpose. They should avoid unnecessary data collection and refrain from using data for purposes beyond what was initially disclosed or consented to. Implementing purpose limitation principles ensures that data is not used in ways that are unexpected or potentially harmful to individuals.

Data Protection and Security Measures: Organizations should implement robust data protection and security measures to safeguard personal data from unauthorized access, breaches, or misuse. This includes using encryption technologies, regularly updating security protocols, and conducting risk assessments to identify and address vulnerabilities. Organizations should also establish incident response plans to effectively respond to data breaches and mitigate their impact.

Ethical Data Analytics and Profiling: When employing data analytics and profiling techniques, organizations should ensure that they are conducted ethically and transparently. This involves avoiding discriminatory practices, ensuring data accuracy, and providing individuals with the opportunity to challenge or contest profiling outcomes. Organizations should also regularly audit and assess the impact of profiling activities to identify and address any potential biases or adverse effects.

Legal and Regulatory Frameworks: Governments should establish clear legal frameworks and regulations that protect privacy and data security. These frameworks should define the rights and responsibilities of individuals and organizations, specify data protection standards, and outline enforcement mechanisms. Governments should also collaborate with international bodies to establish global standards and ensure harmonization of privacy laws across jurisdictions.

Education and Awareness: Promoting privacy education and awareness is essential to empower individuals to make informed decisions about their data. Governments, organizations, and educational institutions should invest in privacy literacy programs to educate individuals about their rights, risks, and best practices for protecting their privacy.

This includes teaching digital literacy, data protection, and privacy-conscious behaviors from an early age.

Privacy and data security concerns pose significant ethical challenges in the digital era. Protecting individuals' privacy requires a collective effort from individuals, organizations, governments, and technology providers. By prioritizing transparency, accountability, and data protection, stakeholders can navigate the complex landscape of privacy and data security, ensuring that individuals' rights are respected while reaping the benefits of technological advancements. Ethical considerations should guide the development of robust privacy frameworks and practices, promoting trust, fairness, and responsible data handling in the digital age.

7.2 Ethical Implications of AI Decision-Making

As artificial intelligence (AI) continues to advance rapidly, its integration into decision-making processes raises important ethical concerns. AI systems have the ability to analyze vast amounts of data, learn from patterns, and make autonomous decisions, potentially impacting various aspects of our lives, including healthcare, finance, criminal justice, and employment. However, the increasing reliance on AI decision-making also raises complex ethical dilemmas, such as bias, accountability, transparency, privacy, and the potential loss of human control. This article delves into the ethical implications of AI decision-making, exploring the challenges and potential solutions for navigating this rapidly evolving landscape.

Bias in AI Decision-Making:

One of the most significant ethical concerns associated with AI decision-making is the potential for bias. AI algorithms are trained on vast datasets, which can inadvertently include biased or discriminatory information. If these biases go unchecked, AI systems can perpetuate and amplify existing social, racial, and gender biases, leading to unjust outcomes. For instance, biased AI algorithms used in hiring processes may discriminate against certain demographics, perpetuating systemic inequalities.

To address this issue, it is crucial to ensure diversity and representativeness in the datasets used for training AI systems. Additionally, ongoing monitoring and auditing of AI systems can help identify and mitigate bias. Developing robust algorithms that are sensitive to bias and incorporating ethical considerations into the design and implementation of AI systems are essential steps toward creating fair and unbiased decision-making tools.

Accountability and Transparency:

AI decision-making often operates as a "black box," meaning that the decision-making process is not always transparent or understandable to humans. This lack of transparency raises concerns regarding accountability and the ability to challenge or question the decisions made by AI systems. Without transparency, it becomes challenging to identify whether an AI system has made an error, exhibited bias, or acted inappropriately.

To address this ethical challenge, there is a need for increased transparency in AI systems. Efforts should be made to develop explainable AI (XAI) models that can provide justifications for their decisions in a way that is understandable to humans. This would enable individuals to contest or seek explanations for AI decisions and hold accountable the entities responsible for deploying and maintaining these systems.

Privacy and Data Protection:

AI systems rely on vast amounts of data to make informed decisions. However, this reliance on data raises significant privacy concerns. The collection, storage, and utilization of personal data for AI decision-making must adhere to strict privacy regulations and ethical principles. Individuals should have control over their data and be made aware of how it will be used in AI systems.

Protecting privacy also includes ensuring that AI systems do not unintentionally disclose sensitive or private information. The development of privacy-preserving AI techniques, such as federated learning and differential privacy, can help address these concerns by enabling data analysis while minimizing the risk of exposing personal information.

Loss of Human Autonomy and Responsibility:

AI decision-making introduces the possibility of humans relinquishing control to machines, raising questions about human autonomy and responsibility. If humans become overly reliant on AI systems to make decisions, there is a risk of abdicating our critical thinking and moral judgment. Additionally, in cases where AI systems make erroneous or harmful decisions, determining responsibility becomes challenging.

It is crucial to strike a balance between the capabilities of AI systems and human involvement in decision-making processes. Humans should retain the ability to oversee and intervene in AI decision-making, particularly in critical domains where ethical considerations are paramount. Establishing clear guidelines and frameworks for human oversight and decision-making in conjunction with AI systems can help mitigate the risk of losing human autonomy.

Unemployment and Economic Inequality:
The integration of AI decision-making systems into various industries can have significant implications

for the workforce. While AI can enhance productivity and efficiency, there is a concern that widespread adoption of AI decision-making may lead to job displacement and exacerbate economic inequality.

AI systems have the potential to automate tasks traditionally performed by humans, leading to job losses in certain sectors. This displacement can have a significant impact on individuals and communities, particularly those who are already marginalized or have limited access to resources and opportunities. The fear is that AI-driven automation may widen the gap between those who possess the necessary skills to work with AI systems and those who do not, further deepening socioeconomic inequalities.

To address these ethical implications, proactive measures must be taken. This includes investing in reskilling and upskilling programs to enable individuals to adapt to the changing job market.

Additionally, fostering an inclusive approach to AI deployment can help ensure that the benefits of AI decision-making are shared equitably, rather than concentrating wealth and opportunities in the hands of a few.

Manipulation and Deception:
AI systems can be programmed to influence human behavior, which raises concerns about manipulation and deception. For example, AI algorithms used in online platforms and social media can be designed to target and manipulate users' preferences, opinions, and even emotions. This raises ethical concerns regarding the autonomy and agency of individuals, as well as the potential for exploitation and abuse.

To address these concerns, there is a need for increased transparency and regulation regarding the use of AI systems for manipulative purposes. Users should have clear information about how AI algorithms are being used to shape their experiences, and there should be mechanisms in place to protect individuals from undue manipulation. Additionally, promoting digital literacy and critical thinking skills can help individuals recognize and navigate potential manipulative practices.

Ethical Decision-Making Frameworks for AI:
To navigate the ethical implications of AI decision-making, the development and adoption of ethical frameworks and guidelines are crucial. These frameworks should encompass principles such as fairness, transparency, accountability, and privacy. They should serve as a roadmap for developers, policymakers, and organizations to ensure that AI systems are designed and deployed in a responsible and ethical manner.

Ethical decision-making frameworks for AI should involve interdisciplinary collaboration and engage stakeholders from diverse backgrounds, including ethicists, technologists, policymakers, and affected communities. It is important to consider a broad range of perspectives and values to ensure that AI systems align with societal norms and aspirations.

As AI decision-making becomes increasingly integrated into various domains, it is essential to address the ethical implications that arise from its deployment. Bias, accountability, transparency, privacy, human autonomy, unemployment, manipulation, and inequality are among the key concerns that need to be carefully considered and addressed.

Addressing these ethical challenges requires a multifaceted approach involving collaboration among researchers, policymakers, industry leaders, and the wider public. Ethical decision-making frameworks, regulations, and guidelines should be developed and implemented to ensure that AI systems operate in a manner that respects fundamental human values and rights.

By proactively addressing the ethical implications of AI decision-making, we can harness the potential of AI while minimizing the risks, ensuring that it serves as a tool for societal benefit and progress. It is through thoughtful consideration, ongoing evaluation, and responsible practices that we can shape AI decision-making to align with our ethical aspirations and promote a fair, just, and inclusive future.

7.3 Human Responsibility in AI Development and Use

Artificial Intelligence (AI) has witnessed remarkable advancements in recent years, permeating various industries and impacting everyday life. From healthcare and transportation to finance and entertainment, AI systems are reshaping how we live, work, and interact. However, as this technology evolves, it brings forth significant ethical considerations that must be acknowledged and addressed.

Transparency and Explainability
Transparency and explainability are vital aspects of AI development and use. Transparency refers to making the decision-making processes of AI systems visible and understandable. Explainability entails providing clear justifications for AI decisions and actions. These aspects are critical for building trust, ensuring accountability, and avoiding the

emergence of "black box" systems that lack transparency.

Human responsibility lies in creating AI systems that are transparent and explainable. Developers and researchers should work towards employing techniques and methodologies that allow for transparency in AI decision-making. Furthermore, they must ensure that AI systems provide explanations that are understandable to non-experts. By involving users and stakeholders in the development process, humans can shape AI systems to be more transparent and accountable.

Fairness and Bias

AI algorithms are trained on vast amounts of data, and if that data is biased, it can perpetuate and amplify existing social biases and inequalities. Human responsibility lies in continuously monitoring and addressing bias in AI development and deployment. This responsibility extends to data collection, data labeling, algorithm design, and the evaluation of AI systems.

Developers must be aware of the potential biases present in the data they use to train AI models. They should strive to collect diverse and representative datasets that reflect the real-world population. Additionally, implementing mechanisms to detect and mitigate bias in AI algorithms is crucial. Regular audits and evaluations should be conducted to identify and rectify any biases that may emerge during the AI system's lifecycle.

Moreover, humans play a significant role in ensuring fairness in AI decision-making. It is essential to establish clear guidelines and ethical frameworks that prevent discriminatory practices and promote equitable outcomes. By actively addressing bias and promoting fairness, we can build AI systems that contribute to a more inclusive and just society.

Accountability

As AI systems become more autonomous and capable of making decisions that have real-world consequences, accountability becomes a paramount concern. It is necessary to identify and allocate responsibility for the actions and outcomes of AI systems. This includes both legal and ethical accountability.

Human responsibility lies in establishing mechanisms to hold individuals and organizations accountable for AI decisions. This could involve regulatory frameworks that outline the responsibilities and liabilities of AI developers, operators, and users. Additionally, ethical guidelines should be developed to guide responsible AI practices and encourage proactive measures to ensure accountability.

Transparency and auditability of AI systems are crucial for accountability. Humans should design AI systems with built-in mechanisms for traceability, enabling the identification of the decision-making processes and the data used. Furthermore, establishing clear lines of responsibility and oversight is essential to ensure accountability throughout the entire AI lifecycle.

Privacy and Data Protection

The widespread use of AI systems often involves the collection and processing of large amounts of personal data. This poses significant risks to privacy and data protection. Human responsibility lies in safeguarding user data and respecting individuals' privacy rights while harnessing the power of AI.

Developers and organizations should adopt privacy-by-design principles, embedding privacy considerations into the development process. This includes implementing robust security measures, obtaining informed consent for data collection and usage, and providing users with control over their data. Additionally, responsible data governance practices, such as anonymization and data minimization, should be prioritized to limit the potential risks associated with AI-enabled data processing.

Regulations and legal frameworks also play a crucial role in protecting privacy in the context of AI. Human responsibility lies in advocating for and complying with privacy laws and regulations that govern AI systems. Balancing the benefits of AI innovation with privacy rights requires a collaborative effort between policymakers, industry stakeholders, and society as a whole.

Safety

AI systems, particularly those with autonomous capabilities, need to operate safely to avoid harm to individuals and society at large. Human responsibility in AI safety encompasses several aspects, including system design, testing, and ongoing monitoring.

Developers have a responsibility to design AI systems that prioritize safety. This involves conducting rigorous testing to identify and mitigate potential risks and vulnerabilities. Safety mechanisms, such as fail-safe mechanisms and redundancy, should be incorporated into the design to ensure that AI systems operate within predefined bounds.

Furthermore, human oversight and monitoring are crucial for ensuring the safety of AI systems. Humans should have the ability to intervene, modify, or shut down AI systems when necessary. Ongoing monitoring and evaluation should be conducted to detect and address safety concerns that may arise during the deployment of AI systems.

Job Displacement

The integration of AI technologies into various industries raises concerns about job displacement and the impact on the workforce. As certain tasks and jobs become automated, it is crucial to address the ethical considerations and responsibilities associated with these changes.

Human responsibility lies in preparing and supporting individuals affected by job displacement due to AI. This includes investing in reskilling and upskilling programs to enable workers to transition into new roles and industries. It is essential to provide opportunities for retraining and education that align with the evolving demands of the job market. Collaboration between governments, educational institutions, and industry stakeholders is crucial to develop comprehensive strategies for workforce transition.

Moreover, humans have a responsibility to ensure that the benefits of AI advancements are equitably distributed. This involves addressing socioeconomic disparities and creating opportunities for individuals who may be disproportionately affected by job displacement. Policies and initiatives that promote inclusive growth, such as universal basic income or job guarantee programs, should be considered to mitigate the negative impacts of AI on employment.

Long-Term Societal Impacts

AI has the potential to reshape society in profound ways, and humans bear the responsibility of shaping its impact to align with our values and long-term goals. It is crucial to consider the broader societal implications of AI development and use, both in the short and long term.

Anticipating and addressing potential risks and unintended consequences of AI is a shared responsibility. Humans should engage in interdisciplinary research and collaborative efforts to understand the societal impact of AI technologies. This involves conducting ethical, legal, and social impact assessments to guide responsible AI development and deployment.

Additionally, ethical decision-making frameworks should be established to guide the development and use of AI systems. These frameworks should encompass principles such as fairness, transparency, accountability, and human well-being. It is important to engage diverse stakeholders, including ethicists, policymakers, technologists, and the general public, in the decision-making process to ensure a wide range of perspectives and values are considered.

Furthermore, long-term planning and proactive measures are necessary to address the potential challenges associated with AI. This includes considering issues such as economic inequality, digital divide, and the impact on democratic processes. Humans should continuously evaluate and adapt AI systems and policies to align with the evolving needs and values of society.

As AI technology continues to advance and become more integrated into our daily lives, human responsibility in its development and use is of paramount importance. Transparency, fairness, accountability, privacy, safety, job displacement, and long-term societal impacts are key areas where humans play a vital role.

By recognizing and addressing these ethical dimensions, we can shape AI systems that align with our shared values and aspirations. Collaboration between researchers, policymakers, industry stakeholders, and the public is essential to ensure responsible AI development and deployment. Through proactive measures, thoughtful decision-making, and continuous evaluation, we can harness the potential of AI while minimizing risks and maximizing the benefits for individuals and society as a whole.

Human-AI Collaboration and Augmentation: Empowering the Future

Advancements in AI have led to a paradigm shift in how we perceive human-AI interaction. Rather than perceiving AI as a replacement for human capabilities, the concept of human-AI collaboration focuses on combining the strengths of both entities to achieve superior outcomes. This collaboration can take various forms, such as augmenting human decision-making processes with AI insights, leveraging AI algorithms to enhance human creativity, or using AI systems to automate mundane tasks and enable humans to focus on higher-level cognitive activities.

Applications of Human-AI Collaboration and Augmentation

2.1 Healthcare

The healthcare sector stands to benefit significantly from human-AI collaboration. AI algorithms can analyze vast amounts of medical data, aiding in disease diagnosis, treatment planning, and personalized medicine. Surgeons can leverage AI-powered robotic systems for precise and minimally invasive surgeries. AI-driven chatbots and virtual assistants can enhance patient care and provide timely medical advice.

2.2 Education

AI technology can revolutionize education by personalizing learning experiences and providing tailored feedback to students. Intelligent tutoring systems can adapt to individual learning styles, identify knowledge gaps, and offer targeted interventions. AI-powered virtual reality simulations can create immersive learning environments, enabling students to engage with complex concepts in a hands-on manner.

2.3 Manufacturing and Industry

Human-AI collaboration has the potential to revolutionize manufacturing processes. AI-powered systems can optimize production lines, predict maintenance needs, and improve quality control. Collaborative robots, or cobots, can work alongside humans, enhancing productivity, safety, and efficiency in industrial settings.

2.4 Creative Industries

AI tools can augment human creativity in various artistic domains. Musicians can leverage AI algorithms to compose novel melodies or assist in music production. Artists can use AI-powered image recognition and generation algorithms to explore new visual aesthetics and create unique artworks.

Benefits of Human-AI Collaboration and Augmentation

3.1 Enhanced Productivity and Efficiency

By leveraging the capabilities of AI systems, humans can offload repetitive and mundane tasks, allowing them to focus on higher-level cognitive activities. This leads to increased productivity and efficiency in various domains.

3.2 Improved Decision Making

AI algorithms can analyze vast amounts of data and extract valuable insights, providing humans with evidence-based recommendations. By augmenting human decision-making processes with AI insights, individuals can make more informed and accurate decisions, minimizing errors and maximizing outcomes.

3.3 Amplified Creativity and Innovation

AI systems can assist humans in generating new ideas, exploring alternative solutions, and pushing the boundaries of creativity. By leveraging AI algorithms, individuals can unlock innovative approaches and break through creative bottlenecks.

3.4 Enhanced Personalization

Human-AI collaboration enables personalized experiences in various fields. From personalized medicine and adaptive learning in education to customized recommendations in e-commerce, AI algorithms can tailor services and products to individual preferences and needs.

Challenges and Ethical Considerations

4.1 Job Displacement and Workforce Adaptation

The integration of AI systems into the workforce raises concerns about job displacement. As AI automates certain tasks, individuals may face the need to adapt their skills to remain relevant in the job market. Addressing this challenge requires proactive efforts in retraining and upskilling the workforce.

4.2 Trust and Transparency

Human-AI collaboration relies heavily on trust between humans and AI systems. Ensuring the transparency of AI algorithms and their decision-making processes is crucial for building trust. Ethical considerations arise when AI systems make decisions that impact individuals' lives, such as in healthcare or legal domains. It is essential to establish clear accountability and transparency frameworks to address these concerns.

4.3 Bias and Fairness

AI algorithms are only as unbiased as the data they are trained on. If training data contains biases, AI systems can perpetuate and amplify those biases, leading to unfair outcomes. It is imperative to mitigate bias in AI systems to ensure fairness and equitable treatment across different demographic groups.

4.4 Privacy and Data Security

Human-AI collaboration involves the exchange of vast amounts of data, raising concerns about privacy and data security. Safeguarding sensitive personal information and ensuring compliance with data protection regulations are crucial to maintain individuals' trust in AI systems.

4.5 Ethical Decision Making and Responsibility

Human-AI collaboration raises questions about ethical decision making and responsibility. When AI systems are involved in decision-making processes, it becomes necessary to establish guidelines and regulations to ensure that the decisions align with ethical standards and human values.

Building Successful Human-AI Collaboration

5.1 Interdisciplinary Collaboration

Successful human-AI collaboration requires interdisciplinary collaboration between experts from various fields, including computer science, psychology, ethics, and domain-specific knowledge. By bringing together diverse perspectives, we can design and implement effective collaboration frameworks.

5.2 User-Centered Design

Developing AI systems with a user-centered approach is crucial for fostering human-AI collaboration. Systems should be intuitive, adaptable, and transparent, catering to users' needs and preferences. User feedback and iterative design processes can enhance the usability and acceptance of AI systems.

5.3 Training and Education

To fully harness the benefits of human-AI collaboration, adequate training and education are necessary. Preparing individuals to work alongside AI systems requires equipping them with the skills to understand, interpret, and leverage AI technologies effectively. This includes critical thinking, data literacy, and ethical reasoning.

5.4 Ethical Guidelines and Governance

Establishing ethical guidelines and governance frameworks is essential to address the ethical considerations associated with human-AI collaboration. Governments, organizations, and researchers need to collaborate in defining ethical standards, ensuring transparency, and promoting responsible use of AI systems.

Future Directions

6.1 Explainable AI

Advancements in explainable AI aim to enhance transparency and interpretability of AI algorithms. By providing understandable explanations for AI decisions, individuals can better trust and collaborate with AI systems.

6.2 Human-AI Hybrid Systems

Future developments may involve the integration of AI directly into the human body or brain, creating human-AI hybrid systems. This raises ethical and philosophical questions about the boundaries between humans and machines, necessitating careful considerations.

6.3 AI for Social Good

Human-AI collaboration can be leveraged to address societal challenges and promote social good. From climate change mitigation to healthcare accessibility, AI systems can assist in finding innovative solutions to complex problems.

6.4 Ethical Frameworks for AI

Continued research and development of ethical frameworks for AI are crucial to guide human-AI collaboration. These frameworks should address fairness, transparency, accountability, and the responsible use of AI in different domains.

Human-AI collaboration and augmentation have the potential to shape the future of various industries and domains. By combining the unique strengths of humans and AI systems, we can achieve unprecedented levels of productivity, creativity, and innovation. However, careful attention must be given to the ethical considerations and challenges associated with this symbiotic relationship. By fostering interdisciplinary collaboration, user-centered design, and responsible governance, we can ensure that human-AI collaboration empowers individuals and society as a whole, while upholding ethical standards and addressing potential risks.

As we move forward, it is essential to strike a balance between leveraging the capabilities of AI systems and preserving human autonomy and agency. Human values, ethical principles, and societal impact should guide the development and deployment of AI technologies. Collaboration between policymakers, researchers, and industry professionals is crucial to establish regulatory frameworks, standards, and guidelines that promote responsible and beneficial human-AI collaboration.

Furthermore, addressing the challenges associated with human-AI collaboration requires ongoing research and development. Innovations in areas such as explainable AI, bias mitigation, and privacy-preserving techniques will contribute to building more trustworthy and transparent AI systems. Continued efforts in education and training will equip individuals with the skills necessary to navigate and leverage AI technologies effectively.

In conclusion, human-AI collaboration and augmentation hold immense promise for shaping the future. By harnessing the strengths of both humans and AI systems, we can achieve unprecedented levels of productivity, efficiency, and innovation across various domains. However, to fully realize the potential of human-AI collaboration, we must address the ethical considerations, challenges, and risks that arise from this symbiotic relationship. With responsible governance, interdisciplinary collaboration, and a focus on human values, we can create a future where AI technologies empower individuals, augment human capabilities, and contribute to the betterment of society.

Ethical Frameworks and Regulations: Guiding Principles for Responsible Conduct

In the digital age, technological advancements have transformed the way we live, work, and interact. However, with the increasing power and influence of technology, ethical considerations have become paramount. Ethical frameworks and regulations provide guidelines to address the ethical dilemmas arising from the use of technology, ensuring that its benefits are harnessed responsibly.

The Importance of Ethical Frameworks
Ethical frameworks serve as a foundation for ethical decision-making, offering a systematic approach to resolve moral dilemmas. These frameworks help individuals and organizations evaluate the potential ethical implications of their actions, enabling them to make informed choices that align with their values. Ethical frameworks promote consistency, transparency, and accountability in

decision-making processes, fostering trust and integrity.

Utilitarianism: The Greatest Good for the Greatest Number

Utilitarianism is a consequentialist ethical theory that emphasizes the maximization of overall happiness or utility. It posits that actions are morally right if they produce the greatest amount of happiness for the greatest number of people. This framework can be applied to technology ethics by considering the potential benefits and harms that arise from technological innovations. However, criticisms of utilitarianism include challenges related to quantifying utility and the potential for minority interests to be overlooked.

Deontology: Duty and Moral Obligations

Deontology, associated with philosophers such as Immanuel Kant, focuses on the inherent duty and moral obligations of individuals. It asserts that certain actions are intrinsically right or wrong, regardless of their consequences. Deontological ethics can guide technology-related decisions by emphasizing the importance of respecting human rights, autonomy, and dignity. However, applying deontological principles to complex technological scenarios can be challenging due to conflicting duties and moral obligations.

Virtue Ethics: Cultivating Moral Character

Virtue ethics shifts the focus from individual actions to the cultivation of moral character. It emphasizes the development of virtues such as honesty, integrity, and empathy, guiding ethical decision-making based on an individual's character rather than adherence to rules or consequences. Applying virtue ethics to technology ethics involves nurturing virtuous behaviors and promoting ethical conduct within technological fields. However, virtue ethics may lack clear guidelines for specific ethical dilemmas, requiring additional frameworks for practical decision-making.

The Role of Regulations in Technology Ethics

While ethical frameworks provide guidelines, regulations play a crucial role in ensuring compliance and accountability. Governments, industry bodies, and organizations establish regulations to protect the rights and interests of individuals, maintain public safety, and address ethical concerns. These regulations encompass a wide range of areas, including data protection, privacy, intellectual property, algorithmic transparency, and responsible AI development. Regulatory frameworks create legal obligations, incentives, and penalties, shaping the ethical landscape of the technology sector.

Challenges in Implementing Ethical Frameworks and Regulations

Implementing ethical frameworks and regulations in the dynamic realm of technology presents various challenges. Technological advancements often outpace the development of ethical guidelines and regulations, creating ethical gaps and dilemmas. The global nature of technology also poses challenges, as regulations differ across jurisdictions, leading to inconsistencies and regulatory arbitrage. Additionally, ensuring compliance and accountability in rapidly evolving fields, such as AI and biotechnology, requires continuous adaptation of ethical frameworks and regulations.

Case Studies: Ethical Frameworks in Practice

Case Studies: Ethical Frameworks in Practice
Examining real-world case studies can provide valuable insights into the application of ethical frameworks and regulations in the technology sector. The following examples illustrate the ethical challenges faced and the approaches taken to address them:

8.1. Data Privacy and Protection: Facebook and Cambridge Analytica

The scandal involving Facebook and Cambridge Analytica highlighted the ethical concerns surrounding data privacy and protection. In this case, Cambridge Analytica harvested personal data from millions of Facebook users without their consent, raising questions about the ethical responsibilities of social media platforms. The incident prompted public outrage and led to increased scrutiny of data privacy practices.

Ethical frameworks such as deontology emphasize the importance of respecting individuals' autonomy and privacy rights. Regulations, such as the European Union's General Data Protection Regulation (GDPR), provide legal safeguards and guidelines for data protection. As a response to the incident, Facebook implemented stricter privacy controls and faced regulatory fines, highlighting the importance of ethical frameworks and regulations in addressing data privacy issues.

8.2. Algorithmic Bias: Discrimination in Automated Systems

Algorithmic bias refers to the unfair or discriminatory outcomes resulting from the use of biased data or flawed algorithms in automated systems. This issue has been particularly prevalent in areas such as hiring, lending, and criminal justice, where algorithms have the potential to perpetuate existing biases and inequities.

Ethical frameworks like utilitarianism call for maximizing overall societal well-being, which includes fairness and justice. Addressing algorithmic bias requires a combination of ethical considerations and regulatory interventions. Efforts have been made to develop guidelines for responsible AI, including the concept of "fairness, accountability, and transparency" (FAT) in algorithmic decision-making. Regulators have also started proposing regulations that aim to mitigate algorithmic bias, ensuring fair and equitable outcomes.

8.3. Autonomous Vehicles: Balancing Safety and Moral Choices

The emergence of autonomous vehicles has raised complex ethical dilemmas, particularly in situations where the technology must make split-second decisions that may have life-or-death consequences. For example, autonomous vehicles may encounter scenarios where they have to choose between saving the passengers or pedestrians in case of an unavoidable accident.

Ethical frameworks like utilitarianism, deontology, and virtue ethics offer different perspectives on how to approach such dilemmas. However, there is no consensus on the "correct" ethical decision. Regulations play a crucial role in setting safety standards and establishing guidelines for autonomous vehicles. They can help ensure that manufacturers and developers consider ethical implications, promote transparency, and conduct thorough risk assessments.

8.4. Intellectual Property: Patenting Genetic Sequences

The field of biotechnology raises unique ethical and regulatory challenges, such as the patenting of genetic sequences. Companies and researchers often seek patent protection for their discoveries, including genes and DNA sequences. However, this practice has sparked debates regarding the ethics of patenting naturally occurring genetic material.

Ethical frameworks such as deontology and virtue ethics emphasize the importance of balancing individual rights, societal benefits, and the common good. Patent regulations, such as the requirement for inventions to be novel, non-obvious, and useful, attempt to strike a balance between incentivizing innovation and ensuring access to genetic information for research and public benefit. Nevertheless, ongoing discussions and legal battles continue to shape the ethical landscape of biotechnology and intellectual property.

Ethical frameworks and regulations are crucial for ensuring responsible conduct in the technology sector. They provide guidelines for decision-making, foster accountability, and address the complex ethical challenges arising from technological advancements. By incorporating ethical frameworks, such as utilitarianism, deontology, and virtue ethics, individuals and organizations can navigate ethical dilemmas and make informed choices. Regulations complement ethical frameworks by providing legal obligations and incentives, promoting compliance, and safeguarding the rights and interests of individuals. As technology continues to evolve, it is essential to adapt and update these frameworks and regulations to keep pace with new challenges and emerging ethical considerations.

Implementing ethical frameworks and regulations in the technology sector does present challenges. The rapid advancement of technology often outpaces the development of corresponding ethical guidelines and regulations. This gap can create ethical dilemmas and uncertainties, requiring ongoing efforts to bridge the divide. Furthermore, the global nature of technology introduces complexities, as regulations and ethical standards may vary across jurisdictions. This can lead to inconsistencies and challenges in ensuring compliance on a global scale.

To address these challenges, collaboration between various stakeholders is crucial. Governments, industry leaders, technology developers, researchers, and ethicists need to work together to develop comprehensive ethical frameworks and regulations. Open dialogue, public consultations, and interdisciplinary collaborations can help establish guidelines that balance innovation with ethical considerations.

Education and awareness are also vital components in promoting ethical behavior. It is essential to cultivate a culture of ethics within the technology sector, ensuring that professionals understand the implications of their work and are equipped with the knowledge to make ethical decisions. Educational institutions, professional organizations, and industry leaders should incorporate ethics training into curricula and provide ongoing professional development opportunities.

Regular evaluation and updates of ethical frameworks and regulations are necessary to address the evolving ethical landscape. Ethical considerations in emerging fields such as artificial intelligence, biotechnology, and autonomous systems require continuous assessment and adaptation of existing frameworks. Additionally, the involvement of diverse perspectives, including those from marginalized communities, is crucial to ensure that ethical frameworks and regulations address the needs and concerns of all stakeholders.

In conclusion, ethical frameworks and regulations are essential components of responsible conduct in the technology sector. They provide guidance and establish standards for ethical decision-making, promote transparency and accountability, and protect the rights and well-being of individuals and society as a whole. By integrating ethical frameworks such as utilitarianism, deontology, and virtue ethics, and implementing robust regulations, we can navigate the ethical complexities of the modern technological landscape and ensure that technology is harnessed for the greater good while respecting fundamental ethical principles.

9.1 Recap of the Argument

Throughout this discussion, we have explored the various dimensions of artificial intelligence (AI) and its implications for society. We have examined both the benefits and risks associated with AI, and considered the potential future perspectives of this rapidly advancing field. Now, it is time to draw conclusions from our analysis and offer recommendations for moving forward.

AI has emerged as a transformative technology that has the potential to revolutionize numerous aspects of our lives. It has already demonstrated remarkable achievements in fields such as healthcare, finance, transportation, and entertainment. AI-powered systems have the capacity to process vast amounts of data, recognize patterns, and make decisions with incredible speed and accuracy. These capabilities have opened up new avenues for innovation, efficiency, and problem-solving.

9.2 Balancing the Benefits and Risks of AI

However, alongside the benefits, there are legitimate concerns surrounding the risks associated with AI. One of the primary concerns is the potential impact on employment. As AI systems become more sophisticated, there is a fear that they may replace human workers, leading to job displacement and economic inequality. It is crucial for policymakers and stakeholders to address these concerns by investing in reskilling and retraining programs to prepare the workforce for the changing nature of work.

Another significant concern is the ethical implications of AI. Issues such as privacy, bias, and accountability need to be carefully considered and regulated. AI systems are only as unbiased and fair as the data they are trained on, and without proper oversight, they can perpetuate societal biases or discriminate against certain groups. It is imperative to establish transparent and accountable mechanisms to ensure that AI technologies are developed and deployed in an ethical and responsible manner.

Furthermore, the potential for AI to be weaponized or used maliciously raises security concerns. As AI becomes more powerful, there is a need for robust cybersecurity measures to protect against potential threats and vulnerabilities. Collaboration between governments, researchers, and industry experts is necessary to establish guidelines and frameworks that promote the responsible and secure use of AI technologies.

9.3 Future Perspectives

Looking ahead, the future of AI holds both exciting possibilities and potential challenges. As AI continues to advance, there will be opportunities for further breakthroughs in areas such as healthcare, climate change mitigation, and scientific research. AI has the potential to enhance medical diagnoses, accelerate the discovery of new drugs, and improve patient outcomes. It can also contribute to addressing global challenges by optimizing resource allocation, predicting natural disasters, and developing sustainable solutions.

However, it is crucial to approach the future of AI with caution and foresight. Policymakers and stakeholders must proactively address the challenges that lie ahead. Collaboration and interdisciplinary approaches are essential for developing robust regulations, standards, and ethical frameworks that guide the development and deployment of AI technologies. Public engagement and education are also vital to foster understanding and awareness of AI's potential and limitations.

Recommendations

Based on the analysis presented in this discussion, several recommendations can be made to balance the benefits and risks of AI and shape its future in a positive direction:

Invest in Education and Training: Governments, educational institutions, and businesses should invest in educational programs and training initiatives to equip individuals with the skills necessary to adapt to the changing landscape of work. Lifelong learning opportunities and reskilling programs can help mitigate the potential negative impact of AI on employment.

Foster Ethical Development and Deployment: Organizations and developers working on AI technologies should prioritize ethical considerations throughout the entire lifecycle of AI systems. This includes promoting transparency, fairness, and accountability, and actively addressing issues such as bias, privacy, and data security.

Establish Regulatory Frameworks: Policymakers should develop comprehensive regulatory frameworks that address the ethical, legal, and social implications of AI. These frameworks should be flexible and adaptable to accommodate the rapid pace of technological advancements while ensuring responsible and accountable use of AI. Regulatory bodies should collaborate with experts from various fields to develop guidelines and standards that promote the responsible development, deployment, and use of AI technologies.

Encourage Interdisciplinary Collaboration: Collaboration between researchers, policymakers, industry experts, and ethicists is crucial for addressing the complex challenges posed by AI. Interdisciplinary collaborations can help foster a holistic understanding of AI's implications and facilitate the development of comprehensive solutions.

Promote Diversity and Inclusion: It is essential to ensure that the development and deployment of AI technologies are inclusive and representative of diverse perspectives and populations. By promoting diversity in AI research teams and considering the needs and perspectives of different communities, we can reduce biases and mitigate the potential harm caused by AI systems.

Foster International Cooperation: Given the global nature of AI and its potential impact, international cooperation is crucial. Governments and organizations should collaborate on establishing common frameworks, standards, and regulations to ensure ethical and responsible AI practices across borders. This includes sharing best practices, exchanging knowledge, and harmonizing policies to address global challenges collectively.

Support Ethical AI Research: Investment in research that focuses on developing ethical AI algorithms, frameworks, and methodologies is essential. By supporting research that addresses biases, privacy concerns, transparency, and accountability, we can promote the development of AI systems that align with societal values and principles.

Continuous Monitoring and Evaluation: As AI technologies evolve, continuous monitoring and evaluation are necessary to identify potential risks, biases, and unintended consequences. Regular audits, assessments, and evaluations of AI systems can help detect and rectify any issues, ensuring ongoing compliance with ethical and regulatory standards.

Foster Public Engagement and Dialogue: Public engagement and dialogue are essential to foster trust, transparency, and understanding regarding AI technologies. Governments, organizations, and researchers should actively engage with the public, seeking their input and addressing their concerns. By involving the public in decision-making processes, we can ensure that AI technologies are developed and deployed in a manner that aligns with societal values and aspirations.

In conclusion, AI presents tremendous opportunities for improving various aspects of our lives, but it also comes with inherent risks and challenges. By balancing the benefits and risks of AI and taking proactive measures, we can shape the future of AI in a way that maximizes its positive impact while mitigating its potential harms. Through investment in education, the establishment of regulatory frameworks, interdisciplinary collaboration, and public engagement, we can promote the responsible and ethical development, deployment, and use of AI technologies. It is crucial that we approach AI with careful consideration, foresight, and a commitment to ensuring that it serves the best interests of humanity.

REFERENCES

Bostrom, N. (2014). Superintelligence: Paths, Dangers, Strategies. Oxford University Press.

Russell, S., & Norvig, P. (2016). Artificial Intelligence: A Modern Approach. Pearson.

Floridi, L. (2019). The Fourth Revolution: How the Infosphere is Reshaping Human Reality. Oxford University Press.

Tegmark, M. (2017). Life 3.0: Being Human in the Age of Artificial Intelligence. Vintage.

Future of Life Institute. (n.d.). Ethics and Governance of Artificial Intelligence. Retrieved from https://futureoflife.org/ai-principles/European Commission. (2019).

Ethics Guidelines for Trustworthy AI. Retrieved from https://ec.europa.eu/digital-single-market/en/news/ethics-guidelines-trustworthy-ai

World Economic Forum. (2018). The Global AI Action Alliance: A Call to Action on Artificial Intelligence. Retrieved from http://www3.weforum.org/docs/WEF_Global_AI_Action_Alliance_CTOs_Call_to_Action.pdf

Partnership on AI. (n.d.). About Us. Retrieved from https://www.partnershiponai.org/about-us/
National Academies of Sciences, Engineering, and Medicine. (2019).

Artificial Intelligence: An International Dialogue. The National Academies Press.

United Nations Educational, Scientific and Cultural Organization (UNESCO). (2021). Recommendation on the Ethics of Artificial Intelligence. Retrieved from https://en.unesco.org/themes/ethics-artificial-intelligence

www.ingramcontent.com/pod-product-compliance
Lightning Source LLC
Chambersburg PA
CBHW032211220526
45472CB00018B/665